ENGLISCH

5.-10. Klasse

English Tenses

Past

Future

ENGLISCH

5.-10. Klasse

Hiltrud Schomaekers
Achim Groß

English Tenses

Die Zeiten

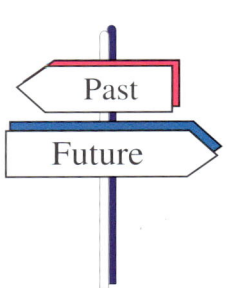

Past

Future

I N H A L T

....

EIN BUCH FÜR ALLE ZEITEN

....

Die Einleitung

Hallo, hier ist MacCool! Auf deinem bevorstehenden Ausflug durch die englischen Zeiten, die **„English Tenses"**, werde ich dein Begleiter sein. Ich bin sicher, daß wir eine Menge Freude vor uns haben, zum Beispiel mit lustigen Rätseln oder mit Übungen, in denen du etwa in die Rolle eines Detektivs schlüpfen und einen Täter finden mußt. Natürlich werden wir beide auch Momente erleben, wo wir einfach müde sind. Dann werden wir gemeinsam ein Päuschen machen – und anschließend geht's weiter mit der **„Weltsprache" Englisch**.

Hast du schon gewußt, daß die englische Sprache **auf allen fünf Kontinenten** zu Hause ist? Oder daß sie Muttersprache von ungefähr 400 Millionen Menschen ist? Sie wird nämlich nicht nur in England und Irland gesprochen, sondern auch in den USA, in Kanada, Australien und Neuseeland. Und in Staaten wie Indien, Kenia oder Südafrika bietet Englisch als Zweitsprache oft die einzige Möglichkeit, sich über Grenzen hinweg zu verständigen.

In sehr vielen Lebensbereichen wie **Wirtschaft, Technik, Sport, Musik, Luft- und Schiffahrt** gilt Englisch längst als Weltsprache Nummer eins. Daher wird sie von so vielen Millionen Menschen als Fremdsprache gelernt und gesprochen. So unwahrscheinlich es klingen mag: 60 Prozent aller Telefonate der Welt werden in Englisch geführt, bei den Briefen sind es sogar 75 Prozent, die in dieser Sprache verfaßt werden.

Die Beherrschung der englischen Sprache ist daher für uns alle wichtig, auch für dich. Und nicht nur im beruflichen Bereich. Sicherlich möchtest du nicht zuletzt die **Texte der Popmusik** besser verstehen, die selbst von deutschen Gruppen häufig in Englisch gesungen werden. Und wenn du ins Ausland reist, egal wohin, kannst du dich mit Englisch immer verständlich machen – auch wenn du die eigentliche Landessprache nicht verstehst.

Die Popmusik ist ohne englische Texte nicht denkbar.

Du lernst die Kultur des jeweiligen Landes besser kennen, du kannst dich mit den Menschen dort unterhalten und sie eher verstehen, du kannst Kontakte knüpfen und Freundschaften schließen. So besteht die Hoffnung, daß mit Hilfe der englischen Sprache die Völker der Erde näher zusammenrücken und keine „Sprachlosigkeit" mehr herrscht.

Das vorliegende Buch **„English Tenses"** soll helfen, dir die **englischen Zeiten** näherzubringen und deine Kenntnisse zu festigen. Auf diese Weise wirst du dich sicher fühlen, wenn du in der Schule Englisch hast oder wenn du mit englisch sprechenden Freunden und Freundinnen zusammentriffst.

Mit Englisch kannst du leicht Freunde aus allen Ländern kennenlernen.

Wer das Buch benutzen sollte …
… alle Schüler und Schülerinnen der Klassen 5 bis 10, aber auch diejenigen der Oberstufe, die Schwierigkeiten mit den englischen Zeiten, den **„English Tenses"**, haben.
Mit Hilfe dieses Buches könnt ihr selbständig Unsicherheiten in der Anwendung beheben, besser noch, ihr braucht Unklarheiten gar nicht erst aufkommen zu lassen.

Was du in diesem Buch findest …
… eine Kombination von Grammatikregeln aller Zeiten und entsprechenden Übungen auf überschaubaren, klar strukturierten Doppelseiten.
Jedes Kapitel ist nach dem gleichen Schema aufgebaut. Als erstes werden dir in leichtverständlichem Deutsch die **Regeln** erklärt. Auf der Randspalte findest du diese Regeln noch einmal kurz zusammengefaßt, damit du dir sie besser einprägen kannst. Es werden stets Vergleiche zur deutschen Zeitenfolge gezogen; ebenso wird auf Unterschiede aufmerksam gemacht.
Im Anschluß daran findest du passende **Übungen** zu den Regeln. Durch die Anordnung der wichtigsten Grundlagen auf einer Doppelseite jeweils kannst du alles Wesentliche zu einer Lerneinheit auf einen Blick erfassen.
Die **Übungen** auf den folgenden Seiten sind in „A" (leicht) und „B" (schwieriger) unterteilt und vielseitig und abwechslungsreich gestaltet. Sie reichen von Einsetzübungen über Rätsel und Dialoge bis hin

Die Regeln und Übungen findest du auf übersichtlich gestalteten Doppelseiten.

zu Aufsätzen und Tests. Auf diese Weise wirst du im Gebrauch der Zeiten immer sicherer. Der **Wortschatz** paßt sich dem Schulenglisch an, so daß du die Vokabeln nicht dauernd nachschlagen mußt und dich völlig auf die Übungen konzentrieren kannst. Mit Hilfe von **Zwischentests** und **Abschlußtests** kannst du selbständig überprüfen, ob du den erarbeiteten Stoff verstanden hast.

Die wesentlichen Elemente einer Doppelseite

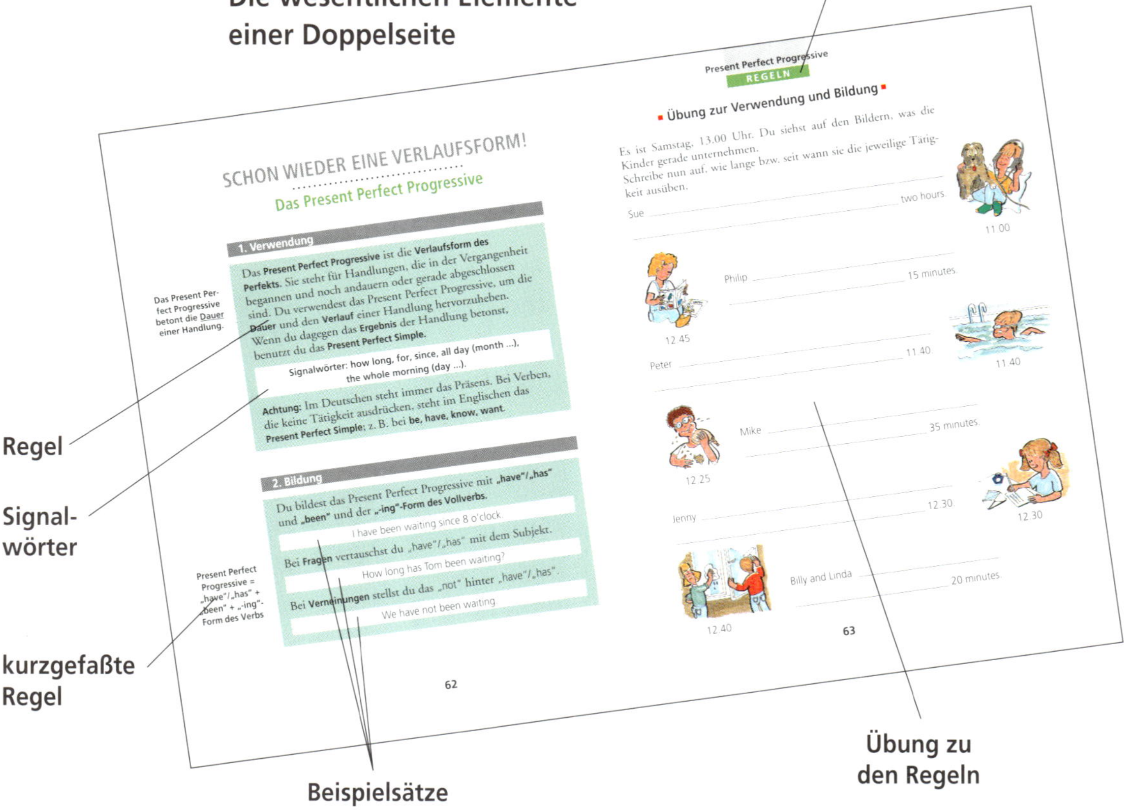

farbiges
Leitsystem

Regel

Signal-
wörter

kurzgefaßte
Regel

Beispielsätze

Übung zu
den Regeln

Present Perfect Progressive
REGELN

▪ Übung zur Verwendung und Bildung ▪

Es ist Samstag, 13.00 Uhr. Du siehst auf den Bildern, was die Kinder gerade unternehmen. Schreibe nun auf, wie lange bzw. seit wann sie die jeweilige Tätigkeit ausüben.

Sue .... two hours
11.00

Philip .... 15 minutes
12.45 .... 11.40
Peter 11.40

Mike .... 35 minutes
12.25
Jenny 12.30
12.30

Billy and Linda .... 20 minutes
12.40

63

SCHON WIEDER EINE VERLAUFSFORM!
Das Present Perfect Progressive

1. Verwendung

Das Present Perfect Progressive betont die Dauer einer Handlung.

Das **Present Perfect Progressive** ist die **Verlaufsform des Perfekts**. Sie steht für Handlungen, die in der Vergangenheit begannen und noch andauern oder gerade abgeschlossen sind. Du verwendest das Present Perfect Progressive, um die **Dauer** und den **Verlauf** einer Handlung hervorzuheben. Wenn du dagegen das **Ergebnis** der Handlung betonst, benutzt du das **Present Perfect Simple**.

Signalwörter: how long, for, since, all day (month ...), the whole morning (day ...).

Achtung: Im Deutschen steht immer das Präsens. Bei Verben, die keine Tätigkeit ausdrücken, steht im Englischen das Present Perfect Simple; z. B. bei be, have, know, want.

2. Bildung

Present Perfect Progressive = „have"/„has" + „been" + -„ing"-Form des Verbs

Du bildest das Present Perfect Progressive mit „have"/„has" und „been" und der „-ing"-Form des Vollverbs.

I have been waiting since 8 o'clock.

Bei Fragen vertauschst du „have"/„has" mit dem Subjekt.

How long has Tom been waiting?

Bei Verneinungen stellst du das „not" hinter „have"/„has"

We have not been waiting

62

Was du mit dem Buch erreichen kannst …
… Die meisten Fehler bei Klassenarbeiten entstehen durch den falschen Gebrauch der Zeiten. Das ist verständlich, weil die englischen Zeiten zum Teil anders gebildet und anders verwendet werden als die entsprechenden deutschen, und es gibt sogar Zeitformen, die im Deutschen gar nicht vorkommen.

Wenn du einzelne Kapitel bzw. das gesamte Buch durchgearbeitet hast, wirst du den Gebrauch der Zeiten besser verstehen und zugleich sicher beherrschen. Dies wiederum bildet die solide Grundlage für gutes Englisch.

1. Wähle das Kapitel aus, das dir besondere Schwierigkeiten bereitet. Du findest es schnell, da im Inhaltsverzeichnis jedem einzelnen Kapitel eine Farbe zugeordnet ist. Im Leitsystem auf jeder Doppelseite rechts oben taucht diese Farbe wieder auf, zusammen mit dem dazugehörigen Kapitel.

2. Arbeite zunächst den Regelteil intensiv durch. Nimm dir genügend Zeit dafür.

3. Löse nun die Übungen auf der jeweils gleichen Doppelseite. Sie beziehen sich stets unmittelbar auf die entsprechenden Regeln.

4. Die Übungen auf den folgenden Seiten sind unterschiedlich schwer. Alle Formen und Verwendungen werden durcheinander abgefragt. Löse die Aufgaben immer schriftlich, teils im Buch, teils im Heft.

5. Schlage anschließend (nicht vorher) im Lösungsteil nach, und überprüfe, ob du die Aufgaben richtig gelöst hast. Markiere etwaige Fehler, und arbeite eventuell das Kapitel noch einmal durch.

Wie du mit dem Buch arbeitest ...

Arbeite **langsam**, aber **regelmäßig** mit dem Buch. Das ist vorteilhafter, als wenn du zum Beispiel vor Klassenarbeiten in Eile ein ganzes Kapitel auf einmal durchnimmst. Du wirst sehen, die Mühe lohnt sich! Und nun viel Glück und Erfolg beim Arbeiten mit den „**English Tenses**".

MacCool

AUF GEHT'S! VIEL SPASS!

DER BEGINN UNSERER ZEITREISE
Das Simple Present

1. Verwendung

Das Simple
Present steht
nach: always,
sometimes,
never, often,
usually, every.

Das **Simple Present** steht im Englischen für die **einfache Gegen-wart**. Du benutzt das Simple Present, um eine Handlung aus-zudrücken, die in der Gegenwart geschieht und regelmäßig ist.

Signalwörter: always, sometimes, never, often, usually, every.

2. Bildung

Das Simple Present ist der Infinitiv oder die erste Form des Verbs. Es wird folgendermaßen gebildet:

I	**like**	ich mag
you	**like**	du magst
he/she/it	**likes!**	er/sie/es mag
we	**like**	wir mögen
you	**like**	ihr mögt
they	**like**	sie mögen

Bei he/she/it
das „s" läuft mit.

Wichtig: Bei **he/she/it** mußt du ein **„s"** anhängen.

Jetzt wollen wir sehen, wie das Simple Present des Hilfsverbs **„be"** („sein") gebildet wird:

I	**am**	ich bin
you	**are**	du bist
he/she/it	**is**	er/sie/es ist
we	**are**	wir sind
you	**are**	ihr seid
they	**are**	sie sind

3. Rechtschreibung

Leider kannst du bei **he/she/it** nicht immer einfach nur ein „s" anhängen, sondern mußt einige Regeln beachten:
Bei allen **Zischlauten (sh, ch, z)** mußt du ein „es" anhängen.

> I teach, *aber* he teach**es**.

Ist der letzte Buchstabe ein „**y**", wird daraus „**ies**", wenn nicht **a, e, i, o, u** vorausgeht.

> He tr**ies**, *aber* he bu**ys**.

Achtung: Es gibt Sonderformen, die man lernen muß!

> Paul **goes**. He **does**.

Bei allen Zisch- lauten steht bei he/she/it „es".

Vorsicht: Sonderformen!

■ Übung zur Verwendung, Bildung ■ und Rechtschreibung

1. Peter _____ to school every morning. 2. Tom and Sandra never _____ their homework together. 3. Your sister _____ ice-cream. 4. I usually _____ at 8 o'clock in the morning. 5. They all _____ to win the bicycle race every summer. 6. Susan sometimes _____ her brother English. 7. Peter's mother always _____ a book in the evening. 8. They often _____ with their Game Boys.

Setze die Verben in der richtigen Reihenfolge und Form in die Lücken ein.

4. Fragen

Fragen bildest du immer mit einem Hilfsverb.

Fragen bildest du **immer** mit einem **Hilfsverb** (z. B.: **can, must, be**).

> Tom must go to school.
> **Must Tom go to school?**

Ist kein Hilfsverb im Satz, mußt du **„do"** oder bei he/she/it **„does"** benutzen. Gebrauchst du „do" oder „does", steht das Verb **immer** im **Infinitiv**.

> I go to school at 7.
> **Do you go to school at 7?**

Fragen mit einem Fragepronomen werden nach derselben Regel gebildet.
Ausnahme: Bei Fragen nach dem Subjekt („who") brauchst du kein Hilfsverb.

Bei „who" kein „do".

> Tina wakes up at 7.15.
> **When does Tina wake up?**
> **Who wakes up at 7.15?**

5. Verneinungen

Verneinung = Hilfsverb + „not"

Wie in der Fragebildung verneinst du einen Satz mit einem **Hilfsverb** und **„not"**.
Ist kein Hilfsverb im Satz, nimmst du **„do not"** oder bei he/she/it **„does not"**.

> I can speak English.
> **My brother cannot speak English.**
> Mother cleans the windows.
> **Father does not clean the windows.**

Kurzformen: „don't"/„doesn't"

Die **Kurzformen** lauten z. B.: **I'm not, you're not, he isn't, she can't, he mustn't, I don't, he doesn't.**
Achtung: must = müssen   must not = nicht dürfen

▪ Übung zur Fragebildung ▪

Lies dir erst einmal jeden einzelnen Satz in Ruhe durch. Frage dann nach den hervorgehobenen Satzteilen. Zweimal mußt du zum gesamten Satz eine Frage bilden. Bei den letzten Sätzen mußt du außerdem die Fragewörter selber finden.

1. Tom goes to school **at 9 o'clock**. **2. Mr Smith** is the trainer of my football team. **3.** Sandra comes from **Liverpool**. **4. Paul and Peter often win bicycle races**. **5. Tom** saves **5 DM** every week. **6.** I buy **a new game** for my Game Boy at the **toy shop**. **7. Every afternoon** Christina must do **her homework**. **8. Peter** washes the car every Saturday. **9. Richard lives in a beautiful house**. **10.** Tanya is **9 years old**.

1. When … ? **2.** Who … ? **3.** Where … ? **4.** … ? **5.** Who … ?

How much … ? **6.** What … ? Where … ? **7.** … ? **8.** … ? **9.** … ? **10.** … ?

▪ Übung zur Verneinung ▪

Verneine die nachfolgenden Sätze.
Beispiel: I go to school at 7 o'clock.
No, I don't go to school at 7 o'clock.

1. My father works in an office. No, my father …
2. You are 5 years old. No, I …
3. The Queen lives in Australia. No, the Queen …
4. Sandra's mother buys a new car every year. No, Sandra's mother …
5. You like English very much. No, I …
6. You can go to school in your summer holidays. No, I …

KEEP COOL! DU SCHAFFST DIE ÜBUNGEN SCHON.

▪ Mister Z ▪

B Mister Z hat in dieser Übung alle Buchstaben der Verben verdreht. Weißt du, wie die Verben richtig heißen? Aber paß auf. Mister Z hat ein Nomen unter den Verben versteckt.

IETRS	_____	EHVA	_____
ACTHE	_____	KTHNI	_____
KILE	_____	MEVRONEB	_____
RIWTE	_____	SYALP	_____

▪ Ein Interview ▪

B Mr Brown, ein Lehrer aus York, ist zu Besuch in Deutschland. Deine Mutter, die kein Englisch spricht, stellt Fragen, die du übersetzen sollst.

1. Mutter: „Was sind Sie von Beruf, Mr Brown?"

You: _____?"

Mr Brown: "I work as a teacher in York."

You: _____

2. Mutter: „Was unterrichten Sie?"

You: _____?"

Mr Brown: "I teach English and History."

You: _____

3. Mutter: „Essen Lehrer und Schüler zu Mittag in der Schule?"

You: _____?"

Mr Brown: "Oh yes, the teachers and pupils have lunch at school,

but I don't."

You: _____

4. Mutter: „Was machen Sie in Ihrer Freizeit?"

You: _____?"

Mr Brown: "I like reading books."

You: _____

5. Mutter: „Arbeitet Ihre Frau auch?"

You: _____?"

Mr Brown: "No, my wife doesn't work."

You: _____

6. Mutter: „Wie gefällt Ihnen Deutschland?"

You: _____?"

Mr Brown: "I like Germany very much."

You: _____

**York:
Schatzhaus
aus dem
17. Jahrhundert**

■ Der Fragebogen ■

A Nun sollst du dir selber einen Fragebogen erstellen. Versuche, Fragen zu bilden. Kreuze anschließend deine Antworten an.

		YES	NO
1.	school / like / you?	☒	☒
2.	clean / your bike / every Saturday / you?	☐	☒
3.	like / this book / you?	☒	☐
4.	read / comics / you?	☒	☐
5.	you / have got / a computer?	☐	☒
6.	have / you / a favourite game?	☒	☐
7.	help / you / at home?	☒	☐
8.	you / go / to school / by bus?	☒	☐
9.	you / help / your mother / your homework / with?	☐	☒
10.	on Saturdays / you / wake up / late?	☐	☐

■ Die Bildergeschichte ■

Erzähle, was Peter **jeden Tag** macht. Die kleine Bildergeschichte hilft **A** dir dabei.

Peter / at 7 / get up.

Mother / breakfast / make.

Peter / by bike / to school / go.

In the afternoon / play / he / with his friends.

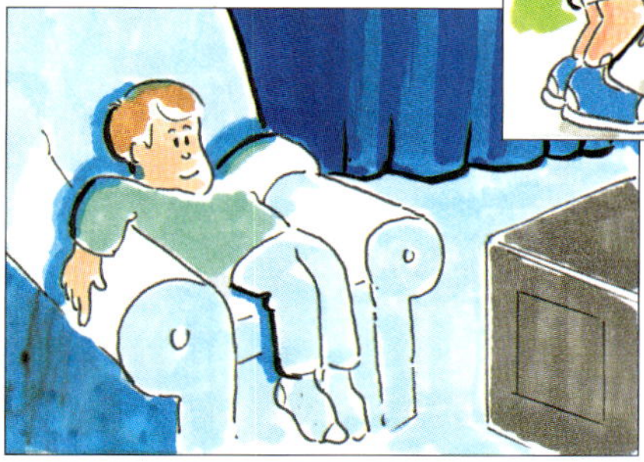

TV in the evening / he / watch.

At 9 / go / he / to bed.

■ Ein Brief ■

Du schreibst einen Brief an deinen Brieffreund oder deine Brief- **B** freundin in England. Du erzählst ihm oder ihr deinen Tagesablauf. Überlege dabei: Wann stehst du morgens auf, wann frühstückst du, was frühstückst du, was lernst du in der Schule, wie lange bleibst du in der Schule …?

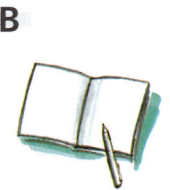

Dear…

17

Hier findest du eine Landkarte von Europa:

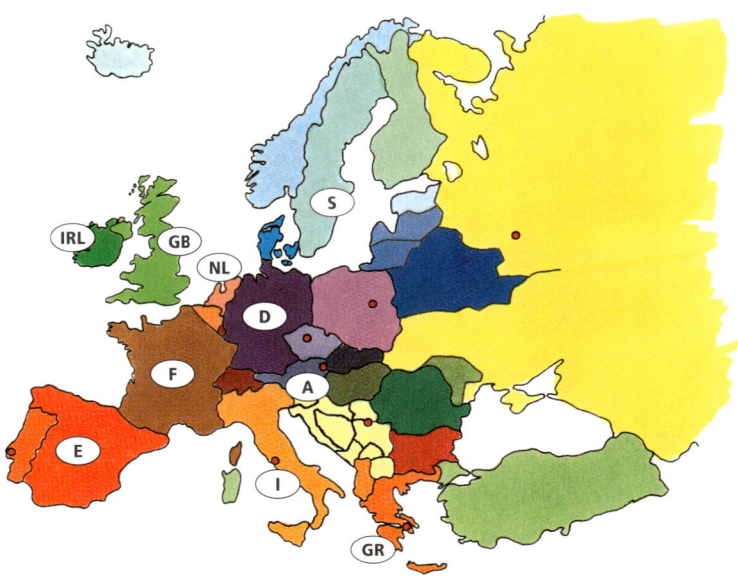

Und hier folgt eine Liste der oben
eingetragenen Länder und der dazugehörigen Sprachen:

GB	English	**1.** Großbritannien = Great Britain
S	Swedish	**2.** Schweden = Sweden
E	Spanish	**3.** Spanien = Spain
F	French	**4.** Frankreich = France
I	Italian	**5.** Italien = Italy
IRL	Irish	**6.** Irland = Ireland
D	German	**7.** Deutschland = Germany
GR	Greek	**8.** Griechenland = Greece
A	German	**9.** Österreich = Austria
NL	Dutch	**10.** Die Niederlande = The Netherlands

Nun wollen wir sehen, ob du dieses Kapitel abschließen kannst.
Oben siehst du eine Karte von Europa mit den wichtigsten Ländern. Darunter findest du die englische Bezeichnung der Länder
und der jeweiligen Sprache. Aus den einzelnen Sprachen stammen
die folgenden Fremdwörter, die du zuordnen sollst.

Beispiel: Does the word **Torero** come from Dutch?
No, it doesn't. It comes from Spanish.

Good luck!

1. Does the word **Jeans** come from French?

   _____

   _____ **2**

2. Does the word **Café** come from Italian?

   _____

   _____ **2**

3. _____ **Computer** _____ Spanish?

   No, it doesn't. It comes from English. **4**

4. Do the words **Souvenir** and **Saison** come from Swedish?

   _____

   _____ **4**

5. Does the word **Foul** come from English?

   _____

   _____ **2**

6. _____ **Paella** _____ from French?

   No, it doesn't. It comes from _____ **2**

7. Do the words **Theater** and **Chemie** come from Irish?

   _____

   _____ **4**

Hast du weniger als 10 Punkte erreicht, solltest du zum Anfang dieses Kapitels zurückgehen und es Schritt für Schritt wiederholen. **20** **Summe**

DIE GEGENWART HAT VIELE GESICHTER

Das Present Progressive (Continuous)

1. Verwendung

Steht „now" und „look" an einem Platz, muß Present Progressive in den Satz.

Das **Present Progressive** steht im Englischen für die **Verlaufsform in der Gegenwart**. Du benutzt das Present Progressive, um eine Handlung auszudrücken, die im Augenblick des Sprechens noch **nicht abgeschlossen**, sondern im Verlauf *(in progress)* ist.

> Signalwörter: Look, now (right now), at the moment ...

Das Present Progressive kann ebenfalls Handlungen ausdrücken, die in der **Zukunft** liegen (Plan / Vereinbarung). Du erkennst dies an einer Zeitangabe oder am Sinn des Satzes. Das Present Progressive steht häufig mit **Tätigkeitsverben.**

Verben der sinnlichen Wahrnehmung <u>nur</u> in der „simple form"!

Achtung: hear, see, smell, taste, be, have, feel, believe, like, want, know, belong to werden **nur** in der *simple form* verwendet.

2. Bildung

Du bildest das Present Progressive mit „be" + „-ing".

Du bildest das Present Progressive mit **„be"** und **„-ing".** Das **„-ing"** hängst du an den Infinitiv des Verbs.

		Kurzformen:
I	am go**ing**	I'm going
you	are go**ing**	you're going
he/she/it	is go**ing**	he's/she's/it's going
we	are go**ing**	we're going
you	are go**ing**	you're going
they	are go**ing**	they're going

3. Rechtschreibung

Leider kannst du nicht immer einfach das „-ing" an den Infinitiv anhängen, sondern mußt Besonderheiten der Schreibweise beachten:

Das stumme „-e" des Infinitivs **fällt weg.**

> I come, *aber* I am co**m**ing.

Stummes „-e" entfällt.

„-ie" am Ende wird **zu „-y".**

> You lie, *aber* you are l**y**ing.

„-ie" wird zu „-y".

Ein **Konsonant** nach einem kurzen Vokal wird **verdoppelt.**

> He runs, *aber* he is ru**nn**ing.

Konsonant wird nach kurzem Vokal verdoppelt.

■ **Übung zur Verwendung, Bildung** ■
und Rechtschreibung

Beschreibe, was die Maus auf den Bildern **gerade** macht.

The mouse …

21

4. Fragen

In einer Frage tauschen „am", „are", „is" und das Subjekt den Platz.

Die Fragebildung ist im Present Progressive viel einfacher als im Simple Present, da ja schon ein Hilfsverb vorhanden ist (am, are, is).
Du **vertauschst** einfach das **Hilfsverb** und das **Subjekt** eines Satzes, um eine Frage zu bilden.

	Fragewort	*Subjekt*	*Hilfsverb*	*Verb*	*Ort*
+		Peter	is	going	to school.
?		Is	Peter	going	to school?
?	Where	is	Peter	going?	

5. Verneinungen

Verneine einen Satz mit „am not", „are not" und „is not".

Auch das Verneinen eines Satzes ist im Present Progressive sehr einfach.
Du **hängst** an das Hilfsverb (am, are, is) ein **„not"** an.

	Subjekt	*Hilfsverb*	*„not"*	*Verb*	*Objekt*
+	Susan	is		helping	her mother.
–	Susan	is	not	helping	her mother.

Achtung: Im Englischen findest du häufig Kurzformen.

Kurzformen: I'm not, you aren't, he / she / it isn't, we aren't, you aren't, they aren't.

Statt **I am not** steht: **I'm not**
Statt **you are not** steht: **you aren't**
Statt **he / she / it is not** steht: **he / she / it isn't**
Statt **we are not** steht: **we aren't**
Statt **you are not** steht: **you aren't**
Statt **they are not** steht: **they aren't**

▪ Übung zur Fragebildung ▪

Auf den Bildern siehst du Personen, die gerade etwas machen. Frage sie, was sie gerade tun, und gib die Antwort.

Beispiel:

"Mother, what are you doing?"
Mother: "I'm cleaning the windows."

"Tim, … "

"Peter, … "

"Grandpa, … "

▪ Übung zur Verneinung ▪

Forme nun die folgenden Sätze in verneinte Sätze um:

1. I'm playing with my Game Boy at the moment.
2. We're playing football now.
3. Mother is cooking lunch today.
4. Father and Tom are washing the car.
5. Look, Peter is doing his homework.
6. My parents are watching TV at the moment.
7. The cat is eating a mouse.
8. I'm cleaning my bike.
9. The girls are singing a song.
10. Sandra is drinking a glass of milk.

Übungen

▪ Die Buchstabensuche ▪

A Im folgenden findest du Verben im Present Progressive, denen ein
Buchstabe fehlt. Suche die fehlenden Buchstaben, und setze sie ein.
Du findest sie auf dieser Seite verteilt.

refer___ing   win___ing   sit___ing   stir___ing

forget___ing   put___ing   run___ing   shut___ing

cancel___ing   cut___ing   get___ing   travel___ing

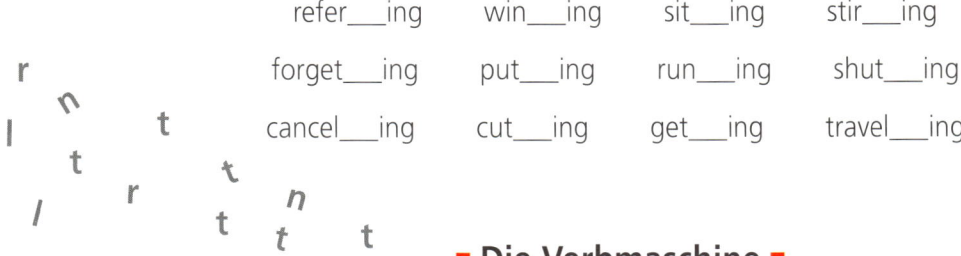

▪ Die Verbmaschine ▪

A Diese Verbmaschine verwandelt die Verben von der Simple Form
in die Progressive Form. Achte auf die Personen.

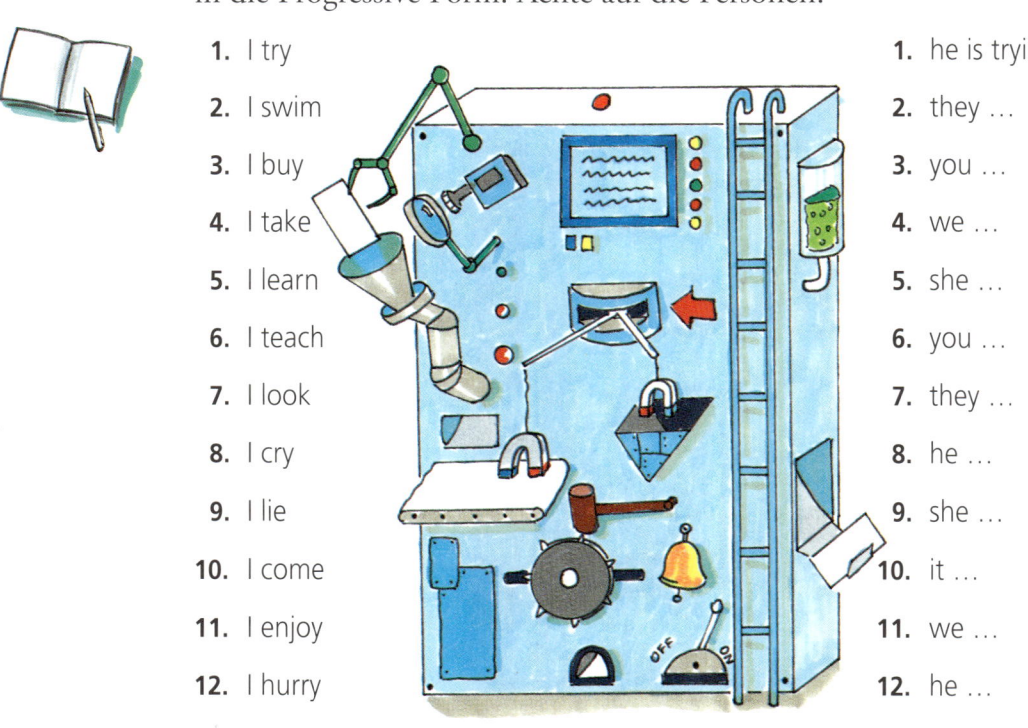

1. I try

2. I swim

3. I buy

4. I take

5. I learn

6. I teach

7. I look

8. I cry

9. I lie

10. I come

11. I enjoy

12. I hurry

1. he is trying

2. they …

3. you …

4. we …

5. she …

6. you …

7. they …

8. he …

9. she …

10. it …

11. we …

12. he …

■ Eine langweilige Hausaufgabe? ■

In der nächsten Übung sollst du nach den hervorgehobenen Satz-   **B**
teilen fragen. Aber gib acht: Manchmal muß eine Entscheidungs-
frage gebildet werden.

Boring Homework
Peter and his friend David are in Peter's room. They're just doing their
English homework. They do their homework together every afternoon.
Suddenly **Peter** hears a **noise**. He jumps up and sees his mother **at the
front door. She** is carrying **big shopping bags**. "What are you doing
there?" David asks. "I can see my mother out there. **She's coming from
the shopping centre**," Peter answers and **runs out of his room**. "If we
finish our homework, we can watch TV later," David shouts. But Peter
doesn't hear David. He hopes his mother has got something to play for
him.
He takes **the shopping bags** and carries them **into the kitchen**. But there
isn't anything for him in the shopping bags, only food.
An hour later David is **watching TV**, and **Peter** is still doing **his homework.**

Beispiel:
1. What are they just doing?
2. Who ...

25

▪ Fragen über Fragen ▪

A Hier findest du nur die Antworten auf Fragen. Kannst du die Fragen bilden?

Beispiel: No, I'm not reading a book at the moment.
Are you reading a book at the moment?

2. Yes, I'm helping my mother in the kitchen. **3.** I'm going to school just now. **4.** Peter is watching TV at the moment. **5.** No, I'm not dancing with Paul this evening. **6.** The cat is lying on the sofa. **7.** Yes, Tom is playing football with his friends. **8.** Because it is raining.

▪ Bildergeschichten ▪

A Beantworte die Fragen zu den Bildern richtig.
Beispiel: Is the boy swimming in the sea?
No, he isn't swimming. He's playing ball.

2. Is the girl playing ball?

3. Are the woman and the man lying in the sun?

4. Is the man drinking a glass of beer?

5. Is one of the girls wearing jeans?

6. Are the girls carrying shopping bags?

7. Are the girls at home?

8. Is one of the girls laughing?

■ Winnetou und Old Shatterhand ■

Versuche nun, diesen kleinen Text ins Englische zu übersetzen.

B

Peter besucht seinen Freund Tom. „Hallo, Tom, was machst du gerade?"
„Ich lese ein spannendes Buch von Karl May (by Karl May)", antwortet
Tom.
„Erzähle mir von dem Buch", sagt Peter. „Im Augenblick bin ich auf
Seite 250. Winnetou und Old Shatterhand reiten in die Prärie und
kämpfen gegen Indianer." „Das ist aber interessant",
sagt Peter. Er fragt Tom: „Kommst du mit? Ich gehe
jetzt in die Bücherei."
„Nein, ich muß noch 150 Seiten lesen", ant-
wortet Tom. Deshalb geht Peter allein in die
Bücherei.

**Vorsicht: Achte
auf die richtige
Zeit!**

■ Der richtige Einsatz ■

A

Setze „is", „are" oder „am" ein.

~~are~~   ~~am~~   ~~are~~   ~~is~~   ~~is~~   ~~are~~   ~~is~~   ~~are~~   ~~am~~   ~~are~~

1. Peter __is__ reading a book now.

2. Tom and Sandra __are__ going to school together.

3. They __are__ playing with their Game Boys.

4. The cats __are__ catching mice.

5. Father __is__ washing his new car.

6. The bird __is__ sitting on the roof.

7. I __am__ cleaning my bike at the moment.

8. We __are__ lying in the sun.

9. I __am__ eating ice-cream.

10. Look, the girls __are__ going to a birthday party.

EIN PRESENT – ZWEI FORMEN

Simple Present und Present Progressive

Wie du schon in den beiden vorigen Kapiteln bemerkt hast, gibt es im Englischen **von jeder Zeit** zwei Formen: *Simple Form* und *Progressive Form.* Dabei gelten **für alle Zeiten** folgende Unterschiede zwischen beiden Formen:

Vergleich

Die Simple Form steht,
▶ wenn man etwas **regelmäßig** tut.
▶ wenn eine Handlung von **Dauer** ist.
▶ bei **„Zustandsverben".**

> want, like, know, belong, love, hate, believe, seem,
> understand, decide, need …

Die Progressive Form steht,
▶ wenn eine Handlung im **Verlauf** ist.
▶ wenn eine Handlung in einem Zeitraum **abläuft.**

Die Simple Form steht z.B. bei „Zustandsverben".

Natürlich kann man den Unterschied an Beispielen viel besser erkennen.

Verwendung der Simple Form

Beispiele für die Verwendung der Simple Form:

1. My father **usually** cuts the grass on Saturdays.
   Mein Vater schneidet **gewöhnlich** samstags den Rasen.

2. The gardener works in the garden.
   Der Gärtner arbeitet im Garten. **(Er ist von Beruf Gärtner.)**

3. My teacher **knows** me very well. **(Zustandsverb: know)**

Beispiele für die Verwendung der Progressive Form:

Verwendung der
Progressive Form

1. Tom is playing with his model cars.
   Tom spielt **gerade** mit seinen Modellautos.
   Die Handlung ist **im Verlauf!**

2. My father is working in the garden **at the moment**.
   Mein Vater arbeitet **im Moment** im Garten.
   Er arbeitet nur **eine bestimmte Zeit** bzw. **in einem bestimmten Zeitraum!**

Um dir bei der Entscheidung zu helfen, welche Zeitform du benutzen mußt, gibt es **Signalwörter,** die häufig im Satz stehen.

Signalwörter des Simple Present:

always, usually, often, sometimes, never, every day,
(week, month, year), in the morning (afternoon)

Signalwörter des Simple Present und des Present Progressive

Signalwörter des Present Progressive:

Look, now, at the moment, just now, right now

■ Top Ten ■

A Gib an, welche Aussage in den folgenden Sätzen gemacht wird.
Schreibe den richtigen Buchstaben in das Kästchen.
Vorsicht: Manchmal ist mehr als eine Lösung möglich.

a = regelmäßig   **b** = Dauer
c = Verlauf   **d** = Zeitraum

1. Your brother plays football very well.   *c*

2. Look, Lothar Matthäus is playing very well.   *c*

3. I'm listening to music now.   *c*

4. Tim usually does his homework in the afternoon.   *a*

5. Jane is walking to work till her car is repaired.   *d/e*

6. Peter speaks two languages.   *b/d*

7. Germany lies north of Switzerland.   *d*

8. Petra isn't wearing jeans today.   *d*

9. He's washing the car at the moment.   *c*

10. The speaker explains why Germany is a member of the EU.   *d*

> BEI **DER** TOP TEN
> GEHT SO RICHTIG
> DER PUNK AB.

▪ Ein Puzzle ▪

Setze die richtigen Puzzleteile zu vollständigen Sätzen zusammen. **A**

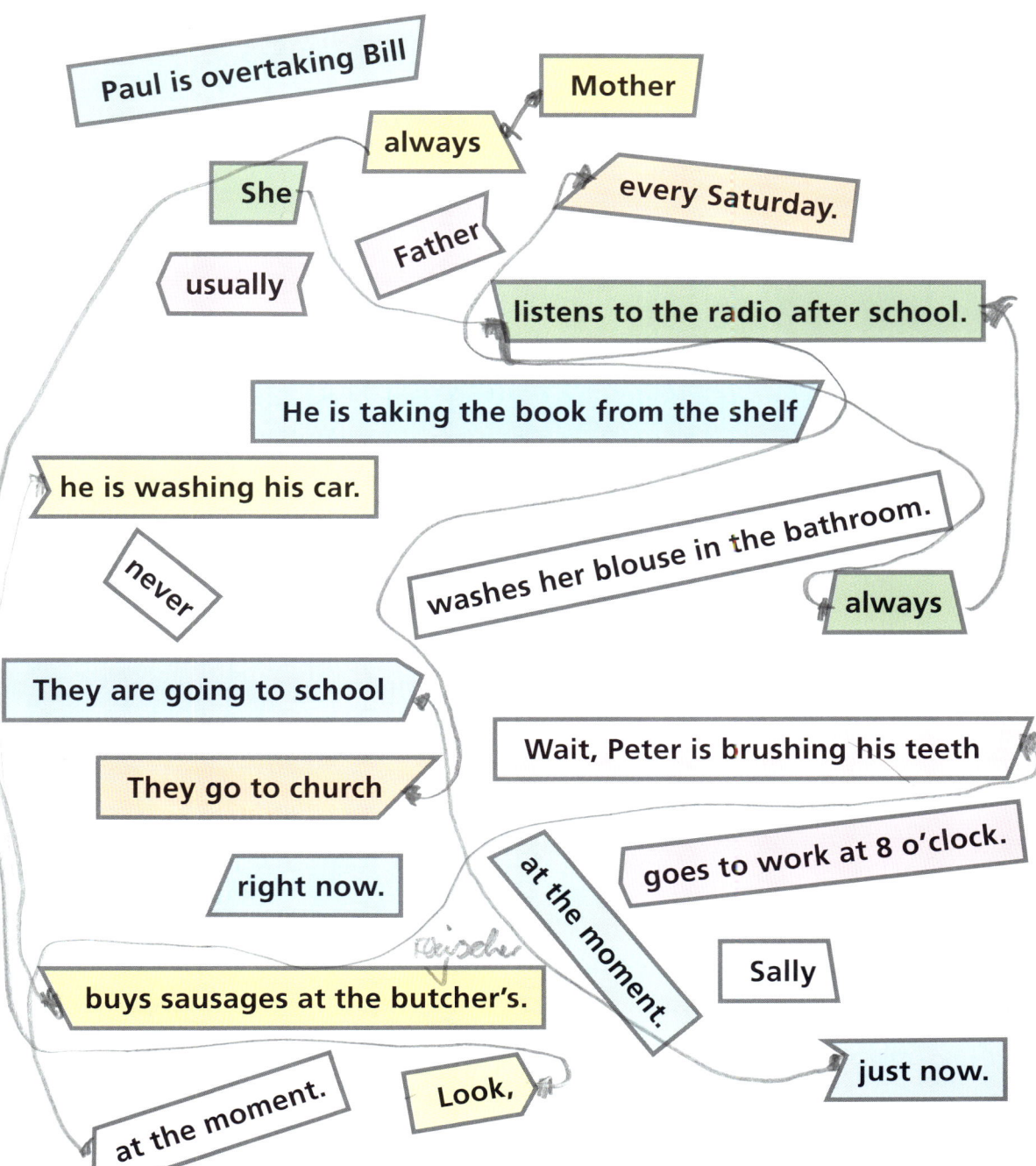

B Dies sind die letzten fünf Minuten einer Radioreportage.
Setze die richtigen Verbformen ein.

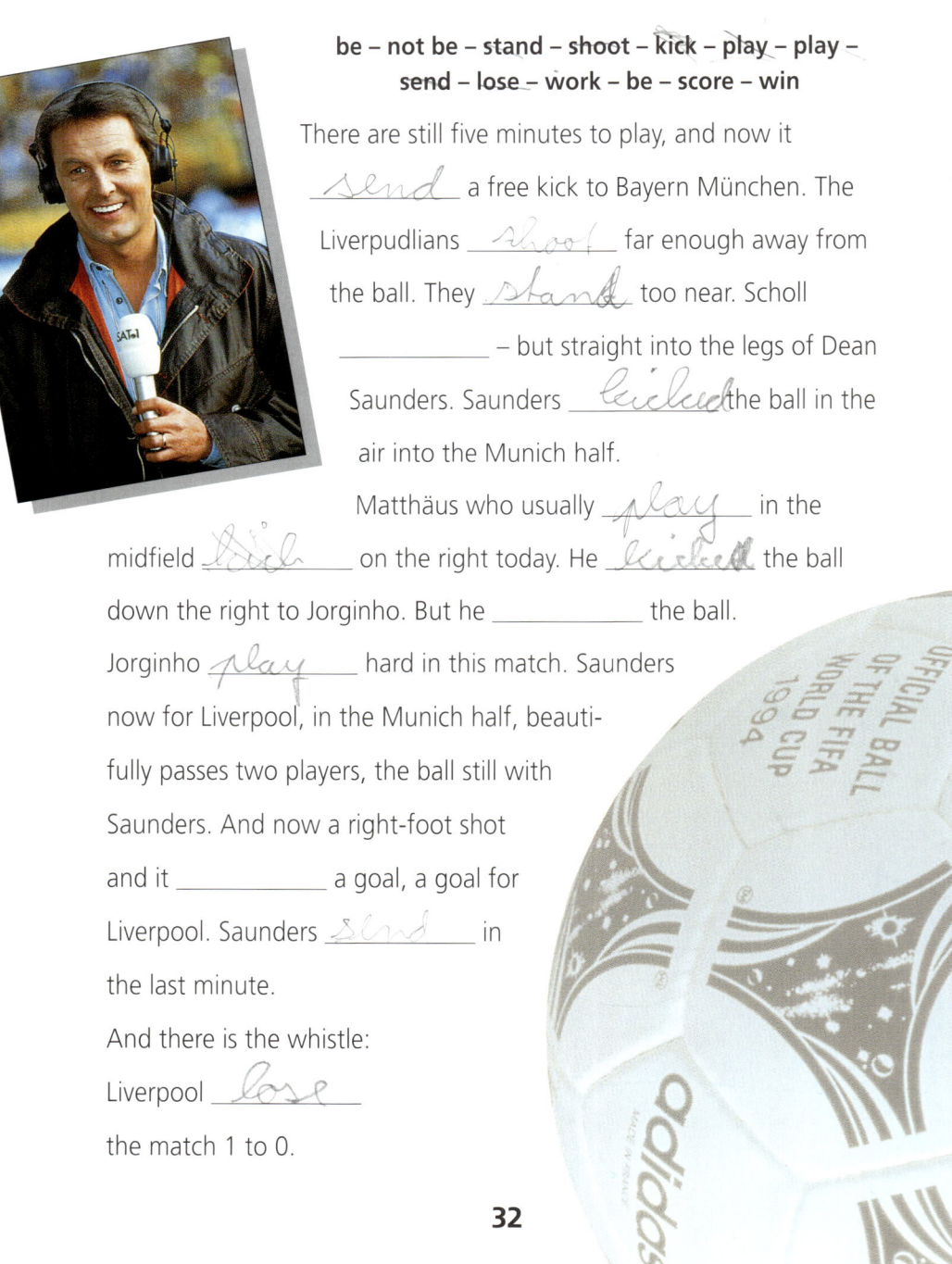

be – not be – stand – shoot – kick – play – play –
send – lose – work – be – score – win

There are still five minutes to play, and now it

send a free kick to Bayern München. The

Liverpudlians _shoot_ far enough away from

the ball. They _stand_ too near. Scholl

_____ – but straight into the legs of Dean

Saunders. Saunders _kicked_ the ball in the

air into the Munich half.

Matthäus who usually _play_ in the

midfield _play_ on the right today. He _kicked_ the ball

down the right to Jorginho. But he _____ the ball.

Jorginho _play_ hard in this match. Saunders

now for Liverpool, in the Munich half, beauti-

fully passes two players, the ball still with

Saunders. And now a right-foot shot

and it _____ a goal, a goal for

Liverpool. Saunders _send_ in

the last minute.

And there is the whistle:

Liverpool _lose_

the match 1 to 0.

32

Test .... **Good luck!**

1. Peter never _____ (brush) his teeth.	**1**
2. Do you sometimes _____ (go) swimming?	**1**
3. Peter _____ (walk) to school till his bike is repaired.	**2**
4. Peter _____ (clean) his shoes at the moment.	**1**
5. It _____ (rain) very little in Africa.	**2**
6. Father's car _____ (look) like new again.	**2**
7. You _____ (like) ice-cream very much.	**1**
8. Honey _____ (taste) sweet.	**2**
9. Because of the bad weather all trains _____ (arrive) late today.	**2**
10. I _____ (go) to the cinema this evening.	**1**
11. Peter _____ (not do) his homework, he _____ (sleep).	**2**
12. This car _____ (cost) 12,000 DM.	**1**
	18 Summe

Hast du weniger als 12 Punkte erreicht, solltest du die Kapitel von Seite 10 an wiederholen.

Zwischentest I

1 Nach den ersten drei Kapiteln dieses Buches möchtest du bestimmt wissen, wie weit du bist.
Nun, dann versuche dein Glück. Im ersten Teil unseres Tests darfst du selber Lehrer spielen. Ein Schüler gibt dir die folgende Klassenarbeit zurück. Kreuze an, ob die Sätze falsch oder richtig sind, und verbessere die Fehler.

Klassenarbeit Nr. 2   **Name:** *Fritz Pechvogel*

		wrong	right
1.	Who does go to school with Peter and Sandra? **(1)**	☒	☒
2.	Peter is never doing his homework alone. **(1)**	☐	☒
3.	He is buying ten bottles of water today. **(1)**	☒	☐
4.	Mrs Belton's house is being at the end of the street. **(1)**	☒	☐
5.	Who goes shopping every morning? **(1)**	☐	☒
6.	Tom and Peter go not swimming. **(1)**	☒	☐
7.	Last year I am in America. **(1)**	☐	☒
8.	It is seeming that Paul is ill. **(1)**	☒	☐
9.	The single fare costs 5 DM. **(1)**	☐	☒
10.	Karl are not going to school this morning. **(1)**	☐	☒
	Summe		**10**

Mark (Note):
mangelhaft

Im zweiten Teil unseres Tests mußt du die Verbformen richtig in die folgende Tabelle einsetzen. Nimm das erste Verb für die 1. Person, das zweite für die 2. Person usw.

2

Simple Present

	Aussagesätze	Verneinungen	
I	write	don't write	
you			2
he/she/it			2
we			2
you			2
they			2
schreiben, nehmen, gehen, fangen, lernen, denken.			

Present Progressive

	Aussagesätze	Verneinungen	
I	am staying	am not staying	
you	are staying	aren't — " —	2
he/she/it	stays	don't stays	2
we			2
you			2
they			2
bleiben, malen, rufen, liegen, aufräumen, stoppen.			20 Summe

Bei weniger als 15 Punkten aus beiden Seiten solltest du die Kapitel von Seite 10 an noch einmal wiederholen.

EINE REISE IN DIE VERGANGENHEIT

Das Simple Past

1. Verwendung

Nach yesterday, ago und last benutze stets das Simple Past.

Das **Simple Past** steht im Englischen für die **einfache Vergangenheit.** Du benutzt das Simple Past für eine Handlung aus der Vergangenheit, die **abgeschlossen ist.**
Wenn du nicht dauernd überlegen willst, ob eine Handlung vorbei ist, helfen dir **Signalwörter,** nach denen **immer** das Simple Past steht:

> yesterday, last *week (month)*, *5 years* ago, in *1972*.

Vergiß nicht: Im Deutschen gebrauchen wir für die Vergangenheit oft das Perfekt.

2. Bildung

Diese Regel gilt auch bei he / she / it.

Bei allen **regelmäßigen Verben** hängst du einfach ein „-ed" an.

> I often work in the garden.
> **Aber:** Yesterday I work**ed** in the garden.

Natürlich gibt es nicht nur regelmäßige Verben, sondern, wie im Deutschen, auch unregelmäßige, die du leider lernen mußt. Das Simple Past der **unregelmäßigen Verben** ist die **zweite Form des Verbs,** die du im *Verzeichnis der unregelmäßigen Verben* findest (siehe Seite 122).

> I always go to school.
> **Aber:** Last week I **went** to school.

■ Übungen zur Verwendung und Bildung ■

The Birthday Present

1

Wandle diese kleine Geschichte ins Simple Past um.

Last month Mike _____ (get) 100 DM from his grandmother as a birthday present. He _____ (be) very happy, because he _____ (want) to buy a mountain bike. He already _____ (have) some money, but it _____ (be not) enough yet, so he _____ (have) to save a bit longer. So that nobody would steal his money, he _____ (put) it into a shoe box with old paper on it and _____ (hide) it under his bed. Every day after school he _____ (take) his money out and _____ (count) it. But when he _____ (come) home one day, the box _____ (be not) there. "Mummy," he _____ (shout), "where is the shoe box?" "That old thing?" his mother _____ (answer), "I _____ (throw) it away. Don't keep so many things in your room!" His mother didn't understand why Mike _____ (be) crying bitterly.

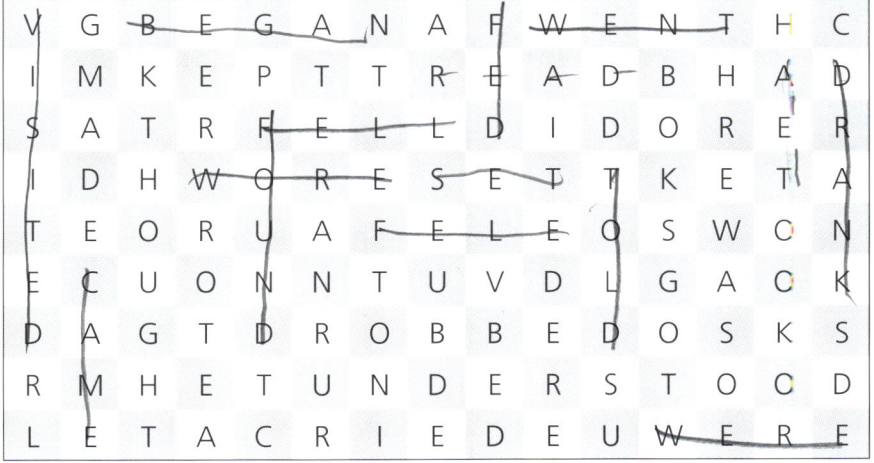

2

In diesem Rätsel sind 33 Vergangenheitsformen versteckt. Um sie alle zu finden, mußt du sie waagerecht und senkrecht lesen. Viel Glück!

V	G	B	E	G	A	N	A	F	W	E	N	T	H	C
I	M	K	E	P	T	T	R	E	A	D	B	H	A	D
S	A	T	R	F	E	L	L	D	I	D	O	R	E	R
I	D	H	W	O	R	E	S	E	T	T	K	E	T	A
T	E	O	R	U	A	F	E	L	E	O	S	W	O	N
E	C	U	O	N	N	T	U	V	D	L	G	A	O	K
D	A	G	T	D	R	O	B	B	E	D	O	S	K	S
R	M	H	E	T	U	N	D	E	R	S	T	O	O	D
L	E	T	A	C	R	I	E	D	E	U	W	E	R	E

3. Rechtschreibung

Bei den regelmäßigen Verben kannst du nicht immer ein „-ed" anhängen, sondern mußt einige **Schreibregeln** beachten: Es wird nur ein **„-d"** angehängt, wenn das Wort schon mit einem **„-e"** endet.

Schreibe nur „-d" bei Wörtern auf „-e".

I like – I liked.

Das **„-y"** nach Konsonanten wird zum **„-i-"**.

Mache das „-y" zum „-i-".

I try – I tried.

Nach kurzem Vokal wird der **Konsonant** am Ende **verdoppelt**.

Verdoppele die Endbuchstaben.

I stop – I stopped.

4. Fragen

▸ Fragen im Simple Past bildest du mit **„did"** und dem **Infinitiv des Vollverbs**.

	Fragewort	„did"	Subjekt	Verb	Ort	Zeit
+			Jimmy	worked	in the garden	yesterday.
?	When	did	Jimmy	work	in the garden	yesterday?

▸ Bei Sätzen mit „was" und „were" brauchst du **kein „did"**.

	Fragewort	Verb	Subjekt	Verb	Ort	Zeit
+			Jimmy	was	in the garden	yesterday.
?	When	was	Jimmy		in the garden?	

Bilde Fragen immer mit „did", außer bei „was", „were", „who".

▸ Fragen nach dem Subjekt *(Wer? Was?)* bildest du ebenfalls **ohne „did"**.

	Fragewort	Subjekt	Verb	Ort
+		Jimmy	worked	in the garden.
?	Who		worked	in the garden?

▪ Übung zur Rechtschreibung ▪

Setze die „Simple-Past"-Formen der regelmäßigen Verben ein:

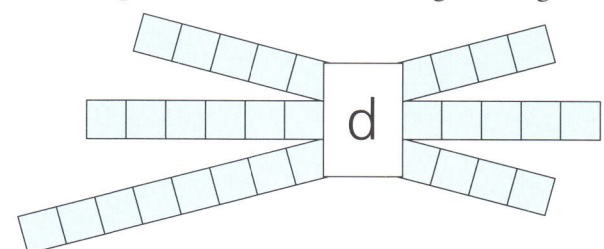

d

| phone |
| carry |
| bake |
| travel |
| rob |
| cry |

▪ Übung zur Fragebildung ▪

Betrachte dir die Bildergeschichte „Bankraub". Stell dir vor, du bist
nun Polizist und mußt den Zeugen folgende Fragen stellen:

1. When / the robber / arrive?
2. What / he / wear?
3. What / to the bank clerk / say / he?
4. Who / the police / call?

5. How many people / be / in
   the bank / there?
6. How much / get / the robber?
7. Where / he / go?

Bei Verneinungen benutze „did not" oder „didn't".

Bei der Verneinung gelten dieselben Regeln wie bei Fragen: Ist kein anderes Hilfsverb im Satz, verneinst du mit **„did not"** oder **„didn't"**. Auch hier steht das Verb im Infinitiv.

	Subjekt	Verb	Ort	Zeit
+	Jimmy	worked	in the garden	yesterday.
–	Jimmy	**didn't work**	in the garden	yesterday.

▪ Übung zur Verneinung ▪

Dein Freund behauptet Dinge von dir, die gar nicht stimmen. Verbessere ihn.

Beispiel: "You went swimming yesterday."
"No, I didn't go swimming yesterday."

1. "You went to the cinema last week."

   "No, I _____"

2. "You lost your mother's money."

   "No, I _____"

3. "You ate a lot of ice-cream."

   "No, I _____"

4. "You drank five glasses of beer yesterday."

   "No, I _____"

5. "You phoned your friend for one hour."

   "No, I _____"

Übungen

▪ Fehlende Verben ▪

Irgend jemand hat in den folgenden Sätzen immer das Verb verges- **A**
sen. Kannst du es einsetzen?

1. Ben ... with his Game Boy yesterday.

2. Tracy ... a letter to her girlfriend Pat last week.

3. Did the police ... the thief two days ago?

4. Kate ... a book about computer games last month.

5. Did Robin Hood ... against the Sheriff of Nottingham?

6. Yesterday my mother ... the windows.

7. The Beatles ... famous pop stars in 1969.

8. ... you buy a bar of chocolate yesterday?

9. Kate did not ... to visit her grandmother last Sunday.

▪ Sommerferien ▪

  **B**

Versuche, eine kleine Geschichte über Toms letzte Sommerferien zu
schreiben. Die Ferien können **(1.)** schön oder **(2.)** scheußlich gewesen sein.
Die folgenden Wörter sollen dir beim Schreiben helfen.
Denke daran, daß du die Geschichte im Simple Past erzählst.

1. wonderful holiday / sun / have fun / go by car / nice camping site / at a lake /
clean / wood nearby / a lot of other children / play football / learn to ride /
lie on the beach / good food.

2. terrible holiday / rain / dirty and noisy camping site / far from a lake / no
children / bad food / fall off the horse / break an arm / hospital.

▪ Drei Briefe ▪

B Hier findest du drei kurze Briefe, die alle einen anderen grammatischen Schwerpunkt haben. Versuche, sie zu übersetzen.

Im Englischen wird das erste Wort nach dem Gruß groß geschrieben.

1. Aussagesätze

Lieber Peter,
gestern hat mich Sandra angerufen. Sie wollte sich ein Buch über Robin Hood ausleihen. Sie hat gestern einen Film über Robin Hood im Fernsehen gesehen und wollte mehr über ihn wissen. Ich fand das Buch sehr interessant und spannend.
Viele Grüße, ...

2. Verneinungen

Liebe Sandra,
gestern bin ich nicht in die Schule gegangen. Ich war krank, habe aber nicht im Bett gelegen. Ich wollte ein Buch lesen, aber es war kein spannendes und interessantes Buch da. Meine Mutter und ich haben darauf gewartet, daß der Arzt kommt. Doch Doktor Müller kam nicht.
Viele Grüße, ...

3. Fragesätze

Liebe Petra,
wo hast du die letzten Sommerferien verbracht? Bist du in die Ferien gefahren, oder bist du zu Hause geblieben? Was hast du den ganzen Tag gemacht? Hast du ein spannendes Buch gelesen? Hat es oft geregnet?
Viele Grüße, ...

·········· **Test** ··········

Auch am Ende dieses Kapitels kannst du wieder überprüfen, ob du alles verstanden hast. Übersetze dazu folgende Sätze:

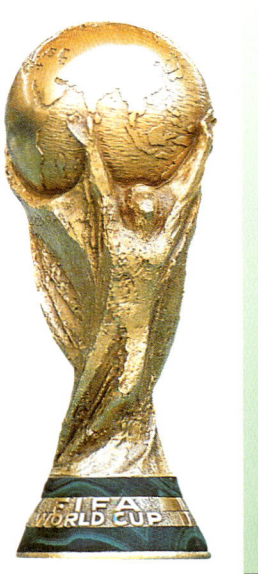

1. Letzte Woche besuchte uns unsere Oma.	1
2. Sie gab mir ein interessantes Buch über Dinosaurier (dinosaurs).	1
3. Kate: „Seid ihr letztes Jahr in die Ferien gefahren?"	2
4. Pat: „Nein, wir sind nicht in die Ferien gefahren."	2
5. Kate: „Was habt ihr gemacht?"	2
6. Pat: „Wir spielten oft mit dem Game Boy, wenn das Wetter schlecht war."	1
7. Gestern abend ging Richard später ins Bett als sein Bruder.	1
8. Vergangenen Samstag gab es einen spannenden (exciting) Film im Fernsehen.	1
9. 1990 gewann Deutschland die Fußballweltmeisterschaft (World Football Championship).	1
10. Vor zwei Stunden habe ich die Übungen in diesem Buch gemacht. Sie waren nicht einfach.	2
	14 Summe

Wenn du weniger als 9 Punkte erreicht hast, solltest du dieses Kapitel wiederholen.

43

WIE KANN EINE ZEIT VERLAUFEN SEIN?
Das Past Progressive

1. Verwendung

Past Progressive = Verlauf

Das **Past Progressive** steht im Englischen für die **Verlaufsform in der Vergangenheit.**
Du benutzt das Past Progressive, um auszudrücken, daß eine Handlung in der Vergangenheit abläuft, während eine andere beginnt.

> While I **was watching** TV, Dad **came** in.

Signalwort: while / when.

2. Bildung

Past Progressive = „was"/„were" + „-ing"

Du bildest das Past Progressive mit **„was"** oder **„were"** und der **„-ing"-Form des Vollverbs.**

> + Tim **was talking** to his friend.
> – The men the police caught **were not wearing** masks.
> ? **Was** the telephone still **ringing**?

Beachte: Für die Rechtschreibung gelten die gleichen Regeln wie beim Present Progressive; z. B.: **coming, trying, swimming.**

ALLE PROGRESSIVE FORMS WERDEN NACH DEN GLEICHEN REGELN GEBILDET.

44

Übung

▪ Wortfetzen ▪

Kannst du die folgenden Wörter zu vollständigen Sätzen ordnen?   **A**

1. came home / I / my parents / when / were reading / the newspaper.

   When _____

   _____

2. his mother / the housework / Peter / had to / while / was doing / his

   homework / do.

   While _____

   _____

3. Sandra's dog / the postman / came / was barking / when.

   When _____

   _____

4. Sam / ready / for school / at eight in the morning / was getting /

   his mother / when / called him.

   _____

   _____

5. Tom's father / an article / all Saturday evening / for the newspaper /

   was writing.

   _____

   _____

6. the accident / was driving / when / happened / who?

   _____

   _____

45

EIN PAST – ZWEI FORMEN

·····································
Simple Past und Past Progressive

Handlungen in der Vergangenheit

Wie du gelernt hast, drücken **beide** Formen – Simple Past und Past Progressive – eine Handlung in der **Vergangenheit** aus.
Doch gibt es Unterschiede in der Anwendung:

Vergleich

Simple Past

Simple Past
1. **Abgeschlossene** Handlung in der Vergangenheit:
   We met him last week.
2. Bei **Zustandsverben:**
   The teacher knew her very well. (siehe Seite 28)
3. **Aufeinanderfolgende** Handlungen in der Vergangenheit:
   Yesterday I woke up, washed and got dressed.

Past Progressive

Past Progressive
1. **Verlauf** einer Handlung in der Vergangenheit:
   Mary was doing the housework all morning.
2. Bei **Tätigkeitsverben:**
   I was writing a letter.
3. Eine Handlung **beginnt,** während eine weitere **im Verlauf** ist:
   While Peter was working, the telephone rang.

DAS MÜSSEN DIE FOLGEN EINER PARTY SEIN.

Übung

■ Die Folgen einer Party ■

Mrs und Mr Miller waren zwei Wochen in Kenia. Bevor sie nach **B** Hause kamen, mußten ihre Kinder Tom und Babs die Wohnung nach einer Party aufräumen. Setze die richtigen Verbformen ein.

First Tom _____ (empty) the ashtrays and the waste-paper

baskets and Babs _____ (carry) out the rubbish. After that,

while Babs _____ (do) the dishes, Tom _____

(clean) the floor.

But while they _____ (hang up) the washing the door bell

_____ (ring). Tom and Babs _____ (get) a terrible

shock when they _____ (hear) it.

They _____ (think) their parents _____ (be) back.

But when Babs _____ (open) the door, she _____

**Ordnung ist das
halbe Leben**

(laugh). The postman _____ (stand) on the doorstep. While

Babs _____ (get) the mail, Tom _____ (come),

because he _____ (want) to know who

_____ (ring) the door bell.

Then Tom _____ (carry) the furniture

back into the living room.

Babs _____ (bake) a cake,

_____ (clean) the kitchen and Tom

_____ (lay) the table.

At 11.00 o'clock they _____ (be) ready.

Everything _____ (be) clean except Tom

and Babs, who _____ (look) very dirty.

Suddenly, while Babs _____ (have) a

shower and Tom _____ (watch) TV, the tele-

phone _____ (ring). Their mother _____ (be) on

the phone and _____ (tell) them that they _____

(want) to stay one more week. Tom and Babs _____ (start) to

laugh and _____ (decide) to have a party again that night.

Test

In den Sätzen sind Fehler versteckt. Finde und markiere sie.
Doch Vorsicht: Es sind zwei richtige Sätze dabei.

1. While Guy Fawkes prepared to blow up the Houses of Parliament some soldiers arrested him in the cellar of the building.	2
2. When the sailors on the English ships noticed the Spanish ships their captain, Sir Francis Drake, was playing bowls.	2
3. In 1990 Germany was winning the World Football Championship.	1
4. Betty was wanting to visit her friend, but he wasn't at home.	1
5. The two men drank together when they suddenly were starting an argument.	2
6. Tim met Sandra at school. They both went to the station.	1
7. When the burglar was seeing the police he tried to run away.	2
8. The teacher was knowing his pupils very well last term.	1

Wenn du weniger als 8 Fehler erkannt hast, solltest du die Kapitel von Seite 36 an wiederholen.	**12** Summe

Zwei torgefähr-
liche deutsche
Nationalspieler
in Aktion:
Rudi Völler und
Jürgen Klinsmann

NOBODY IS PERFECT

Das Present Perfect Simple

Das Present Perfect ist die vollendete Gegenwart.

1. Verwendung

Das **Present Perfect** steht für die **vollendete Gegenwart;** es stellt die Verbindung zwischen Gegenwart und Vergangenheit her. Du benutzt das Present Perfect, um Handlungen oder Vorgänge zu beschreiben,

▸ die **gerade erst** geschehen sind.

▸ die zwar in der Vergangenheit stattfanden, aber **keinen bestimmten Zeitpunkt** nennen. Nur das **gegenwärtige Ergebnis** ist wichtig.

▸ die in der **Vergangenheit begannen** und bis in die **Gegenwart reichen.**

2. Bildung und Rechtschreibung

Das Present Perfect wird <u>immer</u> mit „have"/„has" + 3. Form des Verbs (Past Participle) gebildet.

Du bildest das Present Perfect **immer** mit **„have"/„has"** und der **3. Form des Verbs (Past Participle).** Für das Past Participle hängst du bei den **regelmäßigen Verben** ein **„-ed"** an das Verb.

> I often work in the garden.
> **Aber:** I **have** work**ed** in the garden.

Die Rechtschreibregeln sind ebenfalls die gleichen wie beim Simple Past.
Das Past Participle der **unregelmäßigen Verben** mußt du lernen. Du findest es im *Verzeichnis der unregelmäßigen Verben.*

Siehe Seite 122!

Im Deutschen wird das Perfekt bei einigen Verben mit **„sein"** gebildet, **im Englischen** aber **immer** mit **„have"** oder **„has".**

> Er **ist** angekommen. He **has** arrived.

▪ Übungen zur Verwendung, Bildung ▪ und Rechtschreibung

Hier findest du das Past Participle (die 3. Form) einiger Verben. Schreibe den Infinitiv dahinter. Markiere die regelmäßigen Verben mit einem Kreuz (✗).

1

eaten _____ drunk _____ visited _____

gone _____ seen _____ driven _____

cooked _____ carried _____ written _____

stopped _____ sent _____ bought _____

Vervollständige nun die folgenden Sätze. Benutze dabei immer das Present Perfect.

2

1. My father *has planted a tree* (plant/a tree)
   He is tired now.

2. The boy _____ (lose/mother)
   He is crying now.

3. Mike _____ (wash/car)
   It is clean now.

4. I _____ (live/house/all my life)
   I still live here.

5. Tom _____ (have/bad dream)
   He is afraid now.

6. Anne _____ (do/the dishes)
   She can play now.

7. The plane _____ (take off)
   It is flying to New York.

8. Anne _____ (cut/hair)
   It is short now.

3. Fragen und Verneinungen

Verneinung: „not" hinter „have"/„has"

Frage: Erst „have"/„has", dann Subjekt

Bei der **Verneinung** stellst du das **„not"** einfach **hinter** **„have"/„has"**. Die Kurzform lautet „haven't"/„hasn't". Die **Frage** bildest du, indem du das **Subjekt** mit **„have"/„has"** **vertauschst**.

	Subjekt	„have"/„has"	3. Form	Objekt
+	Jimmy	has	washed	his hands.
?	Has	Jimmy	washed	his hands?
–	Jimmy	has not (hasn't)	washed	his hands.

4. Signalwörter und deren Stellung

Signalwörter des Present Perfect stehen für unbestimmte Zeitangaben.

Folgende **Signalwörter** begleiten **häufig** das Present Perfect:

just	gerade, eben
already	schon (meistens in Aussagesätzen)
yet	schon (in Fragen)
up to now	bis jetzt
so far	bisher
not yet	noch nicht
ever	jemals (häufig in Fragen)
never	noch nie
this morning	diesen Morgen (Abend ...);
(evening ...)	nur, wenn die Zeit schon begonnen hat, aber noch nicht beendet ist

just, already, ever, never stehen unmittelbar vor der **3. Form**, alle anderen Signalwörter am Satzende.

	Signalwort	3. Form	
She has	**just**	cut	the roses.
Have you	**ever**	been	to England?

Aber: Has Jimmy arrived **yet?**

■ Übungen zu Fragen, Verneinungen ■
und Signalwörtern

Bringe die Wörter in die richtige Reihenfolge; verwende dabei das Present Perfect.

1. Australia – to – my – be – never – father
2. We – dinner – not – have – yet
3. Story – Anne – interesting – read – just – an
4. Ever – cricket – play – you?
5. Not – teacher – their – this morning – the pupils – see
6. The car – clean – yet – Tom?
7. Mother – already – the – make – beds – my
8. The – fine – this – weather – be – week

Freddy muß im Haushalt helfen, weil seine Mutter im Krankenhaus ist. Sie ruft ihn an und fragt, was er schon erledigt (√) hat und was noch nicht.
Ergänze das Gespräch:

Mother: "Have you done the washing up yet?"

Freddy: "Yes, I have already done it."

Mother: "Fine, and what about your room?"

Freddy: " _____ "

Mother: " _____ "

Things to do
do the washing up √
tidy room
cook lunch √
clean shoes
finish homework
take dog out √

_____

_____

_____

_____

_____

_____

5. Das Present Perfect mit „since" und „for"

Die Signalwörter für das Present Perfect, **„since"** und **„for"**, stehen immer für Handlungen, die in der **Vergangenheit begannen** und bis zur **Gegenwart andauern**.
Beide Signalwörter bedeuten **„seit"**. Doch kann man sie nicht gegeneinander austauschen.
Merke: *since* = seit und ein bestimmter Zeitpunkt
      for = seit und ein Zeitraum
Ein Tip: Wenn du für „seit" **„lang"** einsetzen kannst, steht **„for"**.

> How long have you been here?
> I have been here for 5 hours (seit 5 Stunden *oder* 5 Stunden lang).
> I have been here since 5 o'clock (seit 5 Uhr).

Achtung: Im Deutschen benutzen wir stets das Präsens.

seit + Zeitpunkt = since
seit + Zeitraum = for

▪ Übung zur Verwendung von „since" und „for" ▪

Setze bei den folgenden Satzteilen „since" oder „for" vor die Ausdrücke.

1. _____ my birthday.

2. _____ three weeks.

3. _____ some minutes.

4. _____ October.

5. _____ 2 o'clock.

6. _____ the last five years.

7. _____ a long time now.

8. _____ our holidays.

9. _____ Christmas.

10. _____ six months.

11. _____ years.

12. _____ I got up this morning.

········· **Übungen** ·········

B ■ **Dein Tagebuch** ■

Denke zurück an den heutigen Tag, und was du
zuvor alles geplant hattest. Schreibe auf, was du
schon getan hast und was noch nicht erledigt
ist.
Wie steht es z. B. mit den Hausaufgaben, mit
dem Einkauf im Supermarkt, mit dem Vogel-
füttern, Autowaschen, Briefmarken kaufen,
Aufräumen …?

■ **Steckverbindungen** ■

Verbinde die Sätze aus der Spalte A mit denen aus der Spalte B. Ver-   **A**
wende für die einzelnen Verbindungen verschiedene Farben.

1 – b / 2 –   / 3 –   / 4 –   / 5 –   / 6 –

A	B
1. Tom is happy.	a. She has eaten too many sweets.
2. My parents are angry.	b. His team has won the match.
3. Sue's face is red.	c. I have lost the car keys.
4. Mary is ill.	d. He has written a good test.
5. Billy is laughing.	e. She has been in the sun all day.
6. My uncle is tired.	f. He has worked very hard.

■ Ein Rätsel ■

B Das folgende Rätsel enthält unregelmäßige Verben. Finde die fehlenden Formen, und trage sie ein.

1. see – saw – …

2. spend – spent – …

3. take – … – taken

4. … – broke – broken

5. eat – ate – …

6. sing – … – sung

7. speak – spoke – …

	7.			
1.	J	O	W	N
2.				
3.	T	O	O	k

4. | B | R | A | K | E |

	5.	E	A	Y	E	N
6.						

8. ride – rode – …

9. ring – … – rung

10. … – won – won

11. give – gave – …

12. … – lost – lost

13. do – did – …

14. drive – drove – …

	14.			
8.	R	I	T	Y	E	N
9.		R	U	N	G
10.	W	I	N
11.	G	I	V	E	N

12. | L | O | S | E |

13. | D | A | N | E |

▪ Eine Ansichtskarte ▪

Peter erhält eine Ansichtskarte, die ihm Freunde aus den Ferien **A** geschrieben haben. Setze „for" oder „since" ein.

Dear Peter,

We have been here _____ 2 weeks now and

_____ Friday the weather has been very fine. We haven't

had such a nice holiday _____ years. We all have been busy

_____ this morning. I have been on the beach

_____ 3 hours and I haven't been so brown

_____ ages.

Betty has written a lot of postcards _____ breakfast and

Tom has been surfing _____ a long time.

That's all for the moment.

Love, _____

▪ Visiting London ▪

B   Martin ist Austauschschüler in London. Er unterhält sich mit seinen englischen Freunden Henry und Sandra. Vervollständige das Gespräch, indem du die fehlenden Wörter richtig einfügst.

Henry: "How long *have you been* (you, be) here?"

Martin: "I _____ (be) here _____ 3 weeks, exactly

_____ 15th August."

Sandra: "_____ you _____ (ever be) to

England before?"

Martin: "No, I have not. This is the first time."

Henry: "_____ you _____ (do) a lot of

sightseeing yet?"

Martin: "Well, I

_____ (already visit) the

Tower and I _____ (take) a boat

trip on the Thames.

That was fantastic."

Sandra: "What about the Houses of

Parliament. _____ you _____ (see) them yet?"

Martin: "No, I _____ (not have) time, and I _____

(not hear) Big Ben either. But I _____

(already climb) to the top of St. Paul's

Cathedral. I had a wonderful view over

London."

Sandra: "Do you like London's parks?"

Martin: "Oh, they are great. I _____ (walk) through Regent's Park lately, and I _____ (look) at the animals in the zoo, I _____ (already listen) to the speakers at Speaker's Corner in Hyde Park twice. I _____ (never hear) such interesting things before."

Henry: "_____ you _____ (ever travel) on a double-decker?"

Martin: "Of course, I _____ (also be) to Buckingham Palace. But the Queen wasn't at home. _____ you _____ (ever meet) her?"

Henry: "Well, we _____ (often see) her – on TV!"

Westminster,
Big Ben

▪ Ein Zeitungsartikel ▪

B Hier findest du einen Artikel, wie er auch in deiner Zeitung stehen könnte. Füge die passenden Verben in die Lücken der Sätze ein.

answer – ask – be – come – do – happen – write

No Money For Traffic Lights?

There _____ (just) another serious accident at Kingsley Corner where a lot of pupils have to cross Queen's Road to get to their school. This year there _____ (already) two deaths here. Therefore parents, children and teachers _____ protest letters to the Council several times and _____ for traffic lights at this corner. But the local authorities _____ yet, and _____ nothing so far. Now the parents think the time _____ to demonstrate against this terrible situation.

Rush-hour in London

60

Test

Übersetze die folgenden Sätze:

1. Mein Bruder hat gerade das Haus verlassen.   **1**

2. Hast du schon Anne angerufen?   **1**

3. Wie lange kennst du deinen Freund?

   Ich kenne ihn seit dem Kindergarten.   **2**

4. Tom ist bis jetzt noch nicht in einem Rockkonzert gewesen.   **1**

5. Wir haben unser Auto schon fünf Jahre.   **1**

6. Mr Miller hat schon sechs Briefe geschrieben.   **1**

7. Mein Großvater ist noch nie nach England gereist.   **1**

8. Das Wetter ist die ganze Woche (bis jetzt) schön gewesen.   **1**

9. Warum ist dein Vater so müde? Er hat den ganzen

   Tag gearbeitet.   **2**

10. Du hast gerade den Test gemacht. Jetzt kannst du spielen.   **2**

                                                                            13   **Summe**

BEI WENIGER ALS 10 PUNKTEN SOLLTEST DU DIESES KAPITEL WIEDERHOLEN.

SCHON WIEDER EINE VERLAUFSFORM!

Das Present Perfect Progressive

1. Verwendung

Das **Present Perfect Progressive** ist die **Verlaufsform des Perfekts.** Sie steht für Handlungen, die in der Vergangenheit begannen und noch andauern oder gerade abgeschlossen sind. Du verwendest das Present Perfect Progressive, um die **Dauer** und den **Verlauf** einer Handlung hervorzuheben. Wenn du dagegen das **Ergebnis** der Handlung betonst, benutzt du das **Present Perfect Simple.**

> Signalwörter: how long, for, since, all day (month ...), the whole morning (day ...).

Achtung: Im Deutschen steht immer das Präsens. Bei Verben, die keine Tätigkeit ausdrücken, steht im Englischen das **Present Perfect Simple**; z. B. bei **be, have, know, want.**

Das Present Perfect Progressive betont die Dauer einer Handlung.

2. Bildung

Du bildest das Present Perfect Progressive mit **„have"/„has"** und **„been"** und der **„-ing"-Form des Vollverbs.**

> I have been waiting since 8 o'clock.

Bei **Fragen** vertauschst du „have"/„has" mit dem Subjekt.

> How long has Tom been waiting?

Bei **Verneinungen** stellst du das „not" hinter „have"/„has".

> We have not been waiting.

Present Perfect Progressive = „have"/„has" + „been" + „-ing"-Form des Verbs

▪ Übung zur Verwendung und Bildung ▪

Es ist Samstag, 13.00 Uhr. Du siehst auf den Bildern, was die Kinder gerade unternehmen.
Schreibe nun auf, wie lange bzw. seit wann sie die jeweilige Tätigkeit ausüben.

Sue _____

_____ two hours.

11.00

Philip _____

_____ 15 minutes.

12.45

Peter _____

_____ 11.40.

11.40

Mike _____

_____ 35 minutes.

12.25

Jenny _____

_____ 12.30.

12.30

Billy and Linda _____

_____ 20 minutes.

12.40

EIN PERFECT – ZWEI FORMEN

....

Present Perfect Simple und Present Perfect Progressive

Verbindung der Vergangenheit mit der Gegenwart

Wie du gelernt hast, betonen **beide** Formen – Present Perfect Simple und Present Perfect Progressive – die Verbindung der **Vergangenheit** mit der **Gegenwart**.

Vergleich

Present Perfect Simple

Present Perfect Simple
1. Diese Form betont das **Ergebnis:**
   She has just painted the picture. (Das Bild ist fertig.)
2. Sie steht bei **Zustandsverben:**
   I have known her for three years. (siehe Seite 28)
3. Sie folgt auf die Frage **how much / how many:**
   I have written three letters.

Present Perfect Progressive

Present Perfect Progressive
1. Diese Form betont das **Andauern** der Handlung:
   Sue's hands are dirty. She has been painting a picture.
   (Das Bild ist noch nicht fertig.)
2. Sie steht bei **Tätigkeitsverben:**
   I have been working for three years.
3. Sie folgt auf die Frage **how long:**
   I have been writing an article all morning.

Übungen

■ Richtig und falsch ■

Wähle die richtige Verbform, indem du die falsche ausstreichst.　　**A**

1. Angela **has found / has been finding** a new job.

2. Mike **has worked / has been working** as a postman for 2 weeks.

3. Mummy, I **have broken / have been breaking** your vase.

4. How long **have you had / have you been having** this car?

5. The tourists **have been visiting / have visited** ten museums today.

6. They **have been travelling / have travelled** around New York all day.

7. Tom **has cut / has been cutting** his finger.

8. **Have you heard / have you been hearing** the latest news?

9. How much money **has she been spending / has she spent** today?

10. How long **have you been reading / have you read** this book?

11. My father **has played / has been playing** „Lotto" for 20 years, but he **has never won / has never been winning** a prize so far.

12. My mother **has been giving up / has given up** smoking.

wrong   right   wrong

right   wrong   right

■ Interview mit einem Popstar ■

B Jim McCawley, ein berühmter Popstar, berichtet in einem Interview über seine Arbeit.
Füge die passenden „Present-Perfect"-Formen in die Lücken der Sätze ein.

I _____ (work) in my job for three years now. I _____

(already produce) ten records and I _____ (win) a prize for two

of them. For the last two weeks I _____ (write) the text

for my next record.

So I _____ (drink) more alcohol than usual and I

_____ (smoke) at least 200 cigarettes for the last five

days. I _____ (not see) much of my family lately,

because we _____ (live) in a village since I became

famous. I _____ (just come) back from a tour

abroad, in fact, I _____ (travel) to many

countries all over the world, and I'm sure all my fans

_____ (enjoy) my music.

Sorry, we have to finish this interview,

because more reporters

_____ (wait) more

than an hour for an

interview.

Test

Übersetze die folgenden Sätze. Überlege dabei, welche Form des Perfekts die richtige ist:

1. Mein Bruder studiert seit zwei Jahren Sprachen an der Universität.   **1**

2. Meine Mutter putzt schon seit 10 Uhr Fenster.   **2**

3. Der Tennisstar spielt seit dem 10. Lebensjahr Tennis.

   Er hat Wimbledon schon viermal gewonnen.   **2**

4. Wie lange sind deine Eltern verheiratet?   **1**

5. Billy arbeitet seit sechs Jahren in London, aber er hat schon

   dreimal die Stelle gewechselt.   **2**

6. Warum sind deine Hände so schmutzig? Ich habe gerade

   mein Auto repariert.   **1**

7. Es schneit schon tagelang, und es hat schon mindestens

   50 cm geschneit.   **2**

8. Mein Freund sucht seit 5 Uhr sein Buch, aber er hat es noch nicht

   gefunden.   **2**

   13   Summe

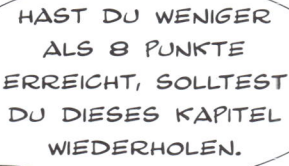

HAST DU WENIGER
ALS 8 PUNKTE
ERREICHT, SOLLTEST
DU DIESES KAPITEL
WIEDERHOLEN.

WIDMEN WIR UNS DEN FEINHEITEN

....

Past Tense und Present Perfect

Die unterschiedliche Verwendung von Past Tense und Present Perfect führt wiederholt zu Fehlern, zumal diese Zeiten im Englischen häufig anders gebraucht werden als im Deutschen. Darum soll an dieser Stelle noch einmal das Wichtigste der beiden Zeiten zusammengefaßt werden.

Verwendung

Signalwörter:
yesterday, ago,
last, when,
in (1960)

Past Tense *(simple und progressive form)*
Das Past Tense bezeichnet Vorgänge, die in der Vergangenheit geschehen und **völlig abgeschlossen** sind. Meistens wird ein **genauer Zeitpunkt** genannt.

Signalwörter:
already, ever,
never, not yet,
since, for, so far

Present Perfect *(simple* und *progressive form)*
Das Present Perfect wird für die Vorgänge gebraucht,
▸ die „**bis jetzt**" geschehen sind,
▸ **ohne** einen bestimmten **Zeitpunkt** zu nennen,
▸ deren Ergebnis aber noch wichtig ist,
▸ oder die in der **Vergangenheit begannen** und in der **Gegenwart** noch **andauern**.

Übungen

■ Der „Lückenfüller"-Test ■

Welche Zeiten sind richtig? Füge sie in die Lücken der Sätze ein. **A**

1. Michael _____ (has been playing; played) tennis for

   3 hours now.

2. Tom _____ (has written; wrote) a letter yesterday.

3. _____ you ever _____ your arm?

   (have – broken; did – break)

4. How long _____ Anne _____ TV?

   (has – been watching; did – watch)

5. When _____ Columbus _____ America?

   (has – discovered; did – discover)

6. We _____ (have bought; bought) our car in 1992.

7. I can't find my glasses. _____ you _____ them?

   (have – seen; did – see)

8. My father _____ never _____ on holiday.

   (has – been; was)

9. _____ you _____ dinner yet?

   (have – had; did – have)

10. Yes, we _____ (have had; had) dinner at 7 o'clock.

▪ Past Tense oder Present Perfect? ▪

B Entscheide, welche der beiden Zeiten du einsetzen mußt. Achte auf die „Progressive"-Formen.

A Long Life

Tim's great grandmother _____ (just celebrate) her

90th birthday. She _____ (be) born in a little village. When she

_____ (be) 10 years old, her family _____ (move) to

a big town and since then she _____ (live) in the same house.

While she _____ (work) in a bank, she _____ (met)

her husband and _____ (marry) him a year later. But he

_____ (die) during the war, and she _____ (never

marry) again. Except for an operation which she _____ (have)

15 years ago, she _____ (not be) seriously ill yet. The reason is

that she _____ (never smoke) and _____ (ride) a bike

since she _____ (be) a child. To keep herself active she

_____ (read) a lot of books and _____ (not miss) the

news on TV so far.

She _____ (have) an interesting life and hopes to live to be a

hundred.

Test

Übersetze die folgenden Sätze:

1. Wann ist der Zug angekommen? Er ist gerade angekommen. 2

2. Wart ihr schon einmal in Italien? Ja, wir haben unsere letzten

    Ferien dort verbracht. 2

3. Mein Vetter ist vor einem Jahr nach Australien gezogen,

    und er hat noch nicht ein Känguruh gesehen. 2

4. Hast du ferngesehen, als ich dich gestern anrief? 2

5. War der Postbote schon hier? Ja, er ist vor fünf Minuten

    hier gewesen. 2

6. Lizzy ist schon fünf Tage im Krankenhaus. Letzte Woche

    hat sie sich ihr Bein gebrochen. 2

7. Wann hast du Alex das letzte Mal getroffen? Ich habe ihn

    seit einer Woche nicht gesehen. 2

8. Vor zwei Monaten hat mein Vater ein Auto gekauft und

    ist schon 2000 km gefahren. 2

9. Gestern abend war ein Gewitter (thunderstorm),

    und seitdem regnet es. 2

10. Hast du schon deine Hausaufgaben gemacht?

    Ja, ich habe sie vor einer Stunde gemacht. 2

Hast du weniger als 12 Punkte erreicht, solltest du nicht weiterarbeiten, sondern erst die Kapitel von Seite 36 an wiederholen. **20 Summe**

....

Zwischentest II

Unser zweiter Zwischentest besteht aus vier Teilen, die die wichtigsten Punkte der bisher erarbeiteten Kapitel zusammenfassen.

| 1 | ■ **Simple Present oder Present Progressive** ■ |

1. I _____ (think) of moving to the USA.

2   What _____ (you think) of it?

2. _____ (you hear) the loud music?

2   It _____ (come) from the party in our neighbourhood.

1   **3.** English pupils usually _____ (have) lunch at school.

4. Peter can't come with us. He _____ (wait) for

1   an important telephone call.

1   **5.** Mother always _____ (do) the shopping on Saturdays.

6. Look, it _____ (rain), and we _____

2   (have not) an umbrella.

Summe   **9**

PST!

72

▪ Simple Past oder Past Progressive ▪   2

1. While Robin Hood _____ (hunt) in Sherwood Forest,

   an arrow _____ (hit) him in his left arm.   **1**

2. When I _____ (wake up) in the morning,

   Mum and Dad _____ (read) the newspaper.   **1**

3. Yesterday my father _____ (wash) his car,

   _____ (paint) the garage, _____ (cut)

   the grass and _____ (buy) a book.   **2**

4. It _____ (seem) that we all _____ (have)

   a lot of fun in our last holidays.   **2**

5. When Columbus _____ (discover) America, the sailors

   _____ (be) all very happy about it.   **1**

6. The telephone _____ (ring) while Mr Becker

   _____ (watch) TV.   **1**

7. In 1900, Victoria _____ (be) Queen of England and the

   British troops _____ (fight) in South Africa.   **1**

8. While Mandy _____ (read) *BRAVO,* her mother

   _____ (come in).   **2**

11 Summe

73

3

■ Simple Past oder Present Perfect ■

2

1. We _____ (have) a lot of rain in May but so far the
   sun _____ (shine) every day this month.

2

2. Where is Sandra? I _____ (not see) her today but she
   _____ (tell) Tim she would come at about 12.00 o'clock.

2

3. _____ (you see) "Hamlet"? No, I _____

2

4. How many English lessons _____ (you have) since the
   beginning of this month?

1

5. Peter and Sandra _____ (visit) some discos since
   last week.

2

6. _____ (you hear) anything about Sandra so far?

1

7. Roman Herzog _____ (be elected) President in 1994.

8. Look, somebody _____ (steal) my bike.

2

   I'll now have to go home by bus.

Summe **14**

SCHON WIEDER
2 PUNKTE!

■ Simple Past oder Past Progressive ■ oder Present Perfect

4

Tim aus Düsseldorf telefoniert mit seinem Freund Peter aus Nürnberg.

Punkte jeweils in Klammern

"Hello, is that you, Peter? Nice to hear you. What _____ (you do) since our last telephone call?" **(2)** "Oh, nice to hear you, too. Do you remember that we _____ (move) to a new house last month? We _____ (not finish) all the work yet. **(3)** Yesterday while I _____ (paint) my room, Mum _____ (come in) and _____ (tell) me that I _____ (have to) go to a new school." **(4)** "Goodness, that sounds very difficult. Over here in Düsseldorf it _____ (rain) for three days now. **(1)** We _____ (not be able to) play outside since then. Last night while I _____ (sleep) there _____ (be) a terrible thunderstorm. I _____ (wake up) and _____ (not be able to) sleep for two hours. **(5)** So I _____ (be) tired this morning. **(1)** Sorry, Peter, my Mum is calling me. I must say good-bye."

Summe   16

Summe Teil 1:	
Summe Teil 2:	
Summe Teil 3:	
Summe Teil 4:	
Summe	50

Hast du insgesamt weniger als 25 Punkte erreicht, solltest du vor dem Weiterarbeiten erst die Kapitel von Seite 36 an wiederholen.

WEITER ZURÜCK GEHT ES NICHT
······························
Das Past Perfect

1. Verwendung

Past Perfect = vorzeitig zum Simple Past

Das **Past Perfect** ist die **vollendete Vergangenheit**. Es beschreibt eine Handlung, die gegenüber dem Simple Past **vorzeitig** ist.

> After Tom had finished his homework,
> (vorzeitige Handlung)
> he played football.
> (Handlung im Simple Past)
> **Signalwörter: after** *und* **before.**

2. Bildung

Past Perfect = „had" + 3. Form

Das Past Perfect wird mit **„had"** und der **3. Form des Vollverbs** gebildet.

> \+ John had finished working in the garage.
> – John had not finished working in the garage.
> ? Who had finished working in the garage?

HIER KANN ICH ETWAS FÜR DIE BILDUNG TUN.

Übungen

▪ Ein Tag mit den Millers ▪

Beschreibe, was den Millers gestern alles passierte. Benutze die folgenden Verben:　　**A**

play, take, watch, go, go to bed, repair, dream, go by bike, do the dishes, go shopping, wake up, have a shower

Beispiel: After Mr Miller had woken up, he had a shower.

Weiter geht's auf Seite 78!

After Mrs. Miller do had done the wishes, she had gone went shopping ✓

77

After Tom Miller had repaired his bike, he had

went by bike to the town.

After Susi Miller had taken photos about the

church, she went back, she went in.

After Lisa and Gregor had played cards, before they had

watched TV.

After Mr Miller had gone to bed, he had

Dies war ein Tag im Leben der Millers … already a dream.

he dreamed about his beautiful wife

■ Paris ■

Tim und John sind Studenten, die sich zum ersten Mal in Paris aufhielten. Hier findest du Aktivitäten aufgelistet, die sie unternommen haben. Verbinde die Sätze.

A

1. arrive at Orly Airport.   2. take a taxi to their hotel.
3. enjoy the view from the Eiffel Tower.
4. make a sightseeing tour to Versailles.
5. go on a boat trip on the Seine.   6. visit the Louvre.
7. take pictures of Paris.   8. return to their hotel.

Beispiel:

1. After they **had arrived** at Orly Airport, they **took** a taxi to their hotel.

2. *After they had taken a taxi to their hotel,*

3. _____
   _____
   _____

4. _____
   _____
   _____

5. _____
   _____

6. _____
   _____

7. _____
   _____

**Ein lange ver-
schollenes
Frühwerk von
Leonardo D.**

■ Die Qual der Wahl ■

B Simple Past oder Past Perfect? Das ist hier die Frage. Entscheide dich für die richtige Form, und setze sie ein.

1. The English test which _____ (come out) last week was

   better than I _____ (expect).

2. The bank clerk _____ (stay) in the bank until the police

   _____ (arrive).

3. This morning Mrs Brown _____ (find) her purse which

   she _____ (lose) three weeks ago.

4. The whole class _____ (be) of the same opinion which

   the teacher _____ (not expect).

5. The police _____ (not understand) how the burglar

   _____ (get) into the house.

6. The old woman _____ (not lock) the front door before

   she _____ (leave) the house.

7. Nobody _____ (seem) to know anything about the film

   which _____ (be shown) yesterday evening.

8. After we _____ (return) from our holidays in Spain

   we_____ (wash) the dirty clothes.

9. When _____ (break out) the

   Second World War _____?

▪ Ein Rätsel ▪

Dieses Rätsel löst du dann richtig, wenn du die Verben in den Klam- **A**
mern ins Englische übersetzt und außerdem das Past Perfect
benutzt. Die Kästchen zeigen die Buchstabenzahl der gesuchten
Verbform an. Die Buchstaben in den hervorgehobenen Kästchen
ergeben in ihrer Reihenfolge ein **Lösungswort.**

1. My brother ▨▨▨ ▨▨▨▨▨ (kaufen) a book about
   computers before he worked with a computer.

2. The eagle ▨▨▨ ▨▨▨▨▨ (ausbreiten) its wings before
   it rose into the air.

3. After Dr. Miller ▨▨▨ ▨▨▨▨▨▨▨▨ (erklären) how
   the medicine should be taken, he gave it to the patient.

4. After our school ▨▨▨ ▨▨▨▨ (brennen) down last year,
   we had to go to a new school.

5. Sandra's dog ▨▨▨ ▨▨▨▨ (beißen) the postman
   yesterday morning before he put the mail into the letterbox.

6. After I ▨▨▨ ▨▨▨▨▨ (reiten) my horse I had to feed it.

7. After the American colonists ▨▨▨ ▨▨▨▨▨ (kämpfen)
   against the British monopoly of tea export to America, war broke out.

8. After the ship ▨▨▨ ▨▨▨ (sinken) a helicopter came to
   rescue the passengers.

9. Mr Miller found the purse he ▨▨▨ ▨▨▨▨ (verlieren) a
   week before.

Lösungswort:

▨▨▨▨▨▨▨▨

■ Ein Fehlertext ■

B Jetzt kannst du wieder einen Fehlertext bearbeiten. Kontrolliere dabei, ob die Sätze richtig übersetzt worden sind. Aber Vorsicht: Es ist auch ein richtiger Satz dabei.

1. Als Mr Smith gestern nach Hause kam, hatte seine Frau schon eingekauft.

   Yesterday when Mr Smith had arrived home, his wife already did the shopping.

2. Es klingelte an der Tür, während Mr Miller duschte.

   The door bell had rung while Mr Miller had a shower.

3. Als Bob zur Bushaltestelle kam, war der Bus schon weg.

   When Bob had come to the bus stop, the bus already left.

4. Sandra brachte Tom einen Kuchen. Sie hatte ihn selber gemacht.

   Sandra brought Tom a cake. She had made it herself.

5. Nachdem Tom nach Hause gekommen war, schaute er Fernsehen.

   After Tom arrived home, he watched TV.

6. Ich sah mir unser Haus an, das wir vor zehn Jahren verkauft hatten.

   I had looked at our house which we sold ten years earlier.

Bist du dem richtigen Satz auf die Spur gekommen, Sherlock Holmes?

······· **Test** ·······

Im folgenden Rätsellabyrinth mußt du deinen Weg Schritt für Schritt mit einer Farbe markieren. Du findest den richtigen Weg nur dann, wenn du alle 3. Formen erkennst.

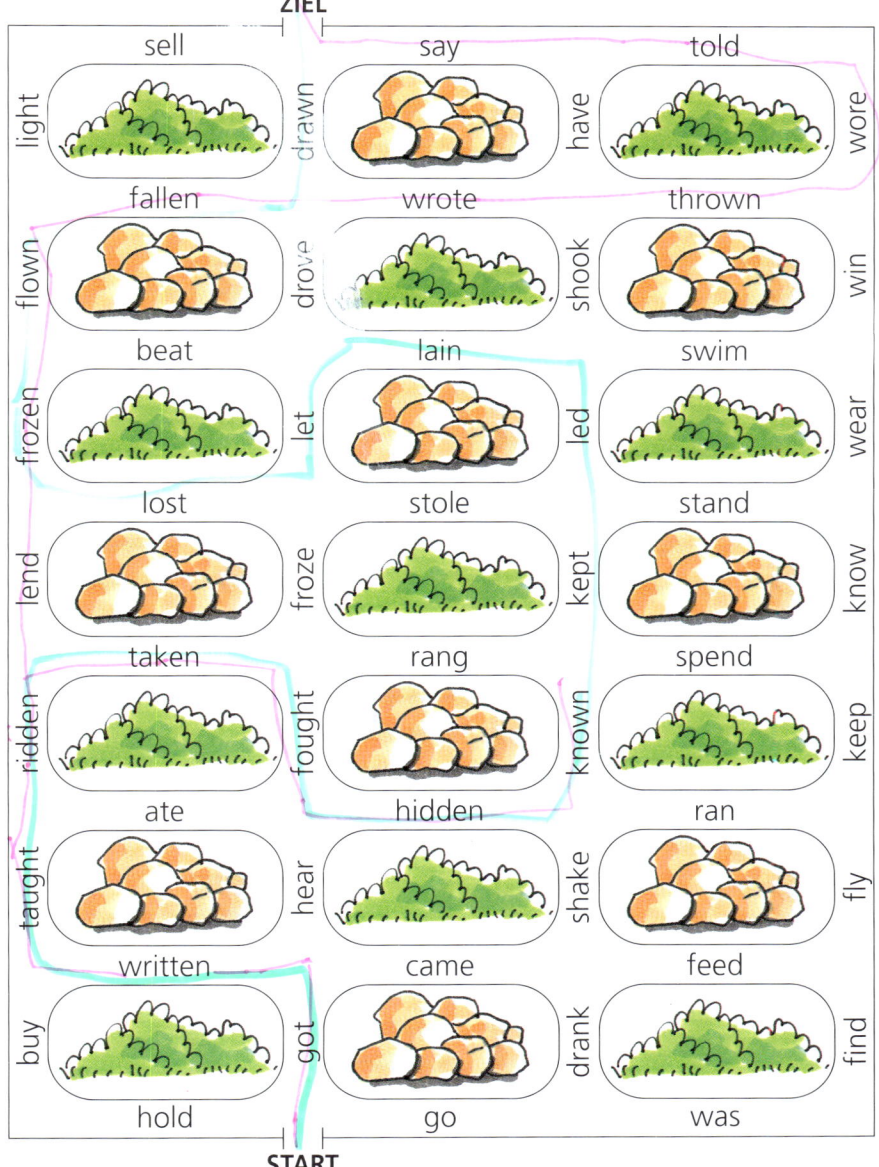

Wenn du am Ziel angelangt bist, kannst du weiterarbeiten.

83

ZEITEN UNTER DER LUPE
···
Past Tense – Present Perfect – Past Perfect

In den folgenden drei Übungen sollst du die richtigen Verbformen herausfinden. Du wirst sehen, daß dies sehr spannend sein kann.

▪ Past Tense, Present Perfect oder Past Perfect? ▪

B

1. I _____ (meet) Tom at the party yesterday evening.

   He _____ (dance) the whole night.

2. The sun _____ (not shine) very often this summer, has it?

3. Before I _____ (start) my car yesterday, I _____ (fasten) the seat belt.

4. Mother thinks it's time to wake up Dad. He _____ (sleep) for 4 hours now.

5. Sorry for being late. How long _____ (you already wait)?

6. After Julius Caesar _____ (die), Augustus _____ (become) emperor.

7. Before England _____ (become) a Republic, Charles I _____ (be executed).

8. Which films _____ (you already see) on TV this week?

9. When Jack and Tina _____ (be) in that little restaurant last week, they _____ (decide) to get married.

▪ Besuch vom Mars ▪

Finde für die folgende Geschichte, die tatsächlich geschehen ist, die richtigen Verbformen heraus. **B**

The Night the Martians Landed

It (be) the evening of October 30th, 1938. Many families (sit) in front of their radios and (wait) for a radio play produced and spoken by Orson Welles. It was the play of the famous novel "The War of the Worlds" by H. G. Wells. The listeners (looking forward to) an hour of excitement but the play (not start). They only (hear) dance music. Suddenly, just when the people (begin) to wonder, an announcer (break) in with the exciting news: "A professor in an observatory (just notice) gas explosions on the planet Mars. A metal spaceship with armed Martians (land) near New

York. 2000 people (be already killed). The Martians (come) to make war on the world." This message (be continued) by an interview with the police. They (order) the announcer to tell the public to remain calm and, if necessary, to defend their country. The news (be told) in such a realistic way that everyone (think) the invasion of the Martians (come) true. People (run) into the streets or into the parks. They (cry) and (shout) for fear and (search) the sky for the Martians. Nobody could believe that it (be) only a radio play. Orson Welles (become) famous for that play all over the world. His version of the "War of the Worlds" (not be forgotten) yet.

▪ Finde den Täter! ▪

B Setze jeweils die richtige Zeit und die richtige Form *(simple* oder *progressive)* ein.

Crime Story

Yesterday evening in Los Angeles. Police cars _____ (stand) in

front of a wonderful bungalow with a swimming pool and a garden near

the seaside. Someone _____ (call) the police 15 minutes ago.

When Inspector Columbo _____ (arrive), he first

_____ (want) to speak to the owner of the house. While he

_____ (enter) the living room, he _____ (see) the

opened and emptied safe. Mr and Mrs Clark, the owner, and their friends,

Mary and Peter Higgins, _____ (sit) and _____ (talk).

"I'm Inspector Columbo," he _____ (say). "What

_____ (happen)?" "When we _____ (come) home,"

Mrs Clark _____ (start), "we _____ (see) the open

front door. First we _____ (think) we _____ (not

lock) it when we _____ (leave) three hours ago. So we

_____ (go) in. But then my husband _____ (see) the

opened safe. After I _____ (call) the police, we

_____ (wait) here since the arrival of the police."

"100,000 dollars and my wife's jewels _____ (be stolen),"

Mr Clark said. "We _____ (be invited) to a large dinner party

with our friends." Peter and Mary Higgins _____ (not say) any-

thing up to now. Inspector Columbo _____ (ask) Peter:

"Is that right, what Mrs Clark _____ (tell) me?"

"Oh yes," Peter _____ (reply), "we _____ (be) at this party, too. Mary _____ (dance) with Mr Clark the whole time, while I _____ (talk) to his wife. We _____ (come) home with the Clarks for a drink at 11.00. After we _____ (enter) the living room, we _____ (see) the safe and Mrs Clark _____ (phone) the police." "What _____ (wear) at that dinner party?" Inspector Columbo asked. "A lot of very famous and important people _____ (be) there, so we _____ (have) to go in evening dress," Mr Clark answered. "But what a silly question!" "Well," Inspector Columbo answered, "now I know the criminal who _____ (steal) the money and the jewels."

Weißt du auch, wer der Täter war? Wenn du dir das Bild genau anschaust, findest du bestimmt den Dieb.

DIE ZUKUNFT KENNT VIELE FORMEN
....
Das will-Future

Um ein zukünftiges Geschehen auszudrücken, gibt es im Englischen **fünf** verschiedene Zukunftsformen. Welche das sind, erfährst du auf den folgenden Seiten. Als erstes das will-Future.

1. Verwendung

Das will-Future steht bei Vorhersagen, Vermutungen, spontanen Entscheidungen.

Du benutzt das will-Future,
▶ um eine **Vorhersage**, eine **Vermutung** oder eine **persönliche Meinung** auszudrücken. *(I think our team will win.)*
▶ um eine **Bitte**, ein **Versprechen** (Zusage) oder eine **spontane Entscheidung**, die du erst im Moment des Sprechens triffst, zu äußern. *(Will you help me? I'll try.)*
▶ um den **Hauptsatz** eines „**if**"-Satzes (Typ 1) zu bilden. *(If it rains, I'll stay at home.)*

„will" + Infinitiv bei allen Personen!

> **Wichtige Signalwörter:**
> I suppose, I expect, I'm sure, perhaps, probably, I hope.

Im Deutschen steht auch bei zukünftigen Handlungen oft das Präsens.

2. Bildung

Du bildest das will-Future mit „**will**" und dem **Infinitiv** (der 1. Form des Verbs). Das gilt für **alle** Personen!

Kurzformen: „will" = „'ll" „will not" = „won't"

> \+ I (you, he ...) will come. I'll (you'll, he'll ...) come.
> – I (you, he ...) will not (won't) come.
> ? Will I (you, he ...) come?

Wichtig: I will = ich werde   I want = ich will

▪ Übung zur Verwendung und Bildung ▪

Die Wahrsagerin Esmeralda antwortet auf die Fragen dieser jungen
Leute immer nur das, was sie gern hören möchten. Sie sagt ihnen
also nur Gutes voraus.
Schreibe die Antworten mit „will" („'ll") oder „won't".

"_____ become a popstar?"

Esmeralda: "You'll become a popstar."

"_____ lose my friend?"

Esmeralda: "Don't worry, _____"

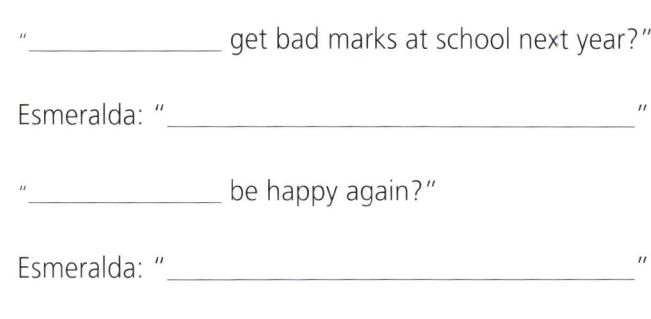

"_____ get bad marks at school next year?"

Esmeralda: "_____"

"_____ be happy again?"

Esmeralda: "_____"

"_____ meet a rich man?"

Esmeralda: "_____"

"_____ our team win?"

Esmeralda: "_____"

"_____ it rain all summer?"

Esmeralda: "_____"

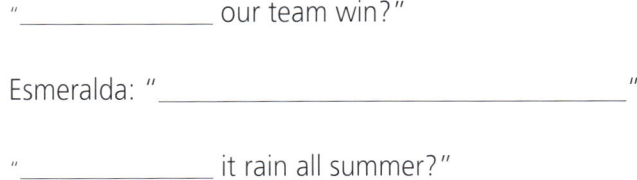

■ Scheinbare Paare ■

A Die folgenden Satzpaare klingen sehr ähnlich, aber nur eine Verbform ist jeweils richtig. Überlege genau, und kreuze die richtige an.

1. That is a beautiful pullover.
a. I buy it for you.
b. I'll buy it for you.

2. What magazine do you read?
a. I read "Bravo".
b. I'll read "Bravo".

3. If the weather is fine,
a. we go swimming.
b. we will go swimming.

4. What time do you eat lunch?
a. We have lunch at 1 p.m.
b. We'll have lunch at 1 p.m.

5. I have lost my money.
a. I lend you some.
b. I'll lend you some.

6. When we get home,
a. I make a cup of tea.
b. I'll make a cup of tea.

7. Whenever Mr Miller gets home,
a. he makes himself a cup of tea.
b. he'll make himself a cup of tea.

8. What would you like to drink?
a. I have a lemonade, please.
b. I'll have a lemonade, please.

■ Blick in die Zukunft ■

B Deine Klasse diskutiert mit eurem Lehrer, wie das Leben in dreißig
Jahren aussieht. Einige Schüler sind Optimisten, einige Pessimisten.
Finde die Fragen, und vervollständige die Antworten mit „will" oder
„won't".

What will life be like in thirty years?

1. *Will schools be better?* (schools/better)

Of course, they _____ be smaller and there _____

be more teachers.

90

I don't agree. There _____ be any school at all, because

pupils _____ learn at home by computers and television.

2. _____? (people / work harder)

I'm sure people _____ work as hard as today, because

robots _____ do most of the work. But I suppose young

people _____ find a job after school and _____

earn less money.

3. _____? (people / more free time)

I imagine people _____ have much more free time. They

_____ fly to the moon for their holiday and _____

travel by helicopter instead of cars. I'm afraid there _____

be any trees, because the air _____ be too dirty.

4. _____? (people / happier)

Yes, I think people _____ be happier than today, because

doctors _____ probably find a medicine against every illness

so that people _____ live longer, and _____ have

to go to hospital.

That's right, but then there _____ be millions more people

in the world, and we _____ have enough to eat.

DAFÜR GIBT ES KEINE ÜBERSETZUNG

Das going to-Future

1. Verwendung

Das going to-Future steht für feste Absichten und kurz bevorstehende Ereignisse.

Du benutzt das going to-Future,

▸ um **feste Vorhaben oder Pläne** für die Zukunft auszudrücken.

> My father hasn't got time now but he's
> going to repair my bike later on.

Aber: Bei spontanem Entschluß steht das will-Future.

> Daddy, my bike is broken. Okay, I'll repair it.

▸ um auszudrücken, daß ein **Ereignis kurz bevorsteht**.
Es gibt schon **Anzeichen** dafür.

> Anne is going to have a baby.

2. Bildung

„am", „are", „is" + „going to" + Verb

Das going to-Future setzt sich zusammen aus dem Präsens von **„be"** (am, are, is) und **„going to"** und dem **Infinitiv** (der 1. Form des Verbs).

> + I **am** (you are / he is …) **going to travel** to America.
> ? Are you (is he …) going to travel?
> – I'm not (you aren't …) going to travel.

Achtung: Bei den Verben „go" und „come" wird das Present Progressive bevorzugt.

> I'm going shopping tomorrow *statt*
> I'm going to go shopping.

■ Übung zur Verwendung und Bildung ■

Es ist Freitag. Die Kinder denken an ihre Pläne fürs Wochenende.
Schreibe, was sie am Wochenende vorhaben. Benutze „going to".

1. Frank _____

_____

2. Lucy _____

_____

3. Peggy and Jenny _____

_____

4. Susan _____

_____

93

▪ „Will" oder „going to"? ▪

A Setze die richtige Zukunftsform ein.
Denke daran: „going to" steht für feste Absichten oder Pläne; sonst benutze „will".

1. Why are you buying so much food? Because I _____

   (cook) for twelve persons.

2. Mother: "I have forgotten to buy milk."

   You: "I _____ (do) that for you."

3. The weather _____ (not be) fine tomorrow.

4. Although my uncle is 64, he _____ (not stop) working next

   year.

5. What _____ your mother _____ (say) when she

   sees your haircut?

6. What would you like to eat, Sir? I _____ (have) soup,

   please.

7. I'm sure Tom _____ (get) the job.

8. If you drop that bottle, it _____ (break).

9. He is very ill; he _____ (die).

10. The tree makes the house very dark. Very well, I _____

    (cut) it down.

11. My parents _____ probably wait for me.

12. _____ you _____ (buy stamps)? Yes, I am. Then

    _____ you buy some for me, please?

▪ Zukunftspläne ▪

Peter hat gerade die Schule beendet. Er schreibt nun seinem Onkel **B**
einen Brief über seine Berufspläne.
Setze „going to" oder „will" ein.

Plans for the Future

Dear Uncle William,

Thank you for your congratulations. I would like to tell you

something about my plans for the future. I _____

(become) a doctor. I haven't decided yet where to study, but

I think I _____ (go) to the University of Cologne,

because a friend of mine _____ (study) there, too.

After my studies I _____ (work) at a hospital. I

suppose I _____ (have) to work hard, but I hope I

_____ (learn) enough to become a good doctor.

Later my friend and I _____ (start) a practice. If we

can save enough money, we _____ (open) a pri-

vate hospital. Maybe my father _____ (lend) us

some money. By the way I _____ (marry) soon. My

future wife _____ (become) a nurse, so she

_____ (probably work) in our practice. I'm sure I

_____ (see) you before I leave for the university.

Love, Peter.

AUCH DIE ZUKUNFT KANN VERLAUFEN

Das Future Progressive

1. Verwendung

Das Future Progressive betont den zukünftigen Verlauf, ein so gut wie sicher eintretendes Ereignis oder eine höfliche Anfrage.

Du benutzt das Future Progressive,

▸ um zu betonen, daß eine Handlung zu einer bestimmten Zeit in der Zukunft **ablaufen wird.**

> This time tomorrow I will be flying to America.

▸ um auszudrücken, daß ein zukünftiges Ereignis **so gut wie sicher eintreten wird.**

> I'll be going shopping in the afternoon.

▸ um **höflich** nach den **Plänen** und **Wünschen** anderer zu fragen.

> Will you be inviting the Smiths?

Auch hier gilt: Die „Progressive"-Form kannst du nur mit Tätigkeits- oder Vorgangsverben bilden.

2. Bildung

„will be" + „-ing"-Form bei allen Personen!

Kurzformen: „'ll be" und „won't be"

Du bildest das Future Progressive mit **„will ('ll) be"** und der **„-ing"-Form des Vollverbs.**
Das gilt wiederum für **alle** Personen!

> + I will (I'll) be waiting.
> − I will not (won't) be waiting.
> ? Will you be waiting?

▪ Übung zur Verwendung und Bildung ▪

Herr Schmidt ist ein vielbeschäftigter Bankmanager in Frankfurt am Main. Hier ist ein Auszug aus seinem Terminkalender:

Wednesday 7th July	
1. 8 a.m. – 9.30 a.m.	fly to London
2. 10.30 a.m. – 11.30 a.m.	visit the Bank of England
3. 1 p.m.	have lunch at the Hilton
4. 2 p.m. – 4 p.m.	discuss financial problems with English bankers
5. 5 p.m.	have an interview with the BBC
6. 8.30 p.m.	leave for Frankfurt

Schreibe, was Herr Schmidt tun wird.

1. From 8 a.m. – 9.30 a.m. he will be flying to London.

2. Between _____

_____

3. _____

_____

4. _____

_____

5. _____

_____

6. _____

_____

DIE ZUKUNFT HAT SCHON BEGONNEN

....

Präsensformen mit zukünftiger Bedeutung

Das Present Progressive steht für die nahe Zukunft.

Ähnlich wie das going to-Future benutzt du das **Present Progressive** (nur bei Tätigkeits- und Vorgangsverben), um über bereits **festgelegte Pläne**, **Vereinbarungen** oder **Verabredungen** in der **nahen Zukunft** zu sprechen. Ob das Present Progressive die Gegenwart oder die Zukunft ausdrückt, muß aus dem Zusammenhang oder aus einer Zeitbestimmung der Zukunft hervorgehen **(soon, tomorrow, this week, next Sunday ...).**

> I'm painting my room tomorrow (*Zukunft*).
> I'm painting my room (*im Augenblick*).

.... **Übungen** ....

▪ Satzbau ▪

A   Bilde Sätze im Present Progressive.

1. Bill / fly / to London / this weekend.
   Bill is flying to London this weekend.
2. My sister / get married / in August.
3. Go / your brother / to Paris / tomorrow?
4. Henry / play / tennis / with Anne / this afternoon.
5. He / leave / for Hamburg / next week.
6. We / not watch / TV tonight.
7. My uncle / come / to see us / next Friday.
8. You / not go / on holiday / this summer.
9. We / do / our English homework / in an hour's time.

■ Wochenendpläne ■

Bob und Lucy sind Arbeitskollegen und unterhalten sich über das
Wochenende. Vervollständige das Gespräch. Benutze das Present
Progressive.

B

Weekend Plans

Bob: "What _____ you _____ (do) this weekend,

Lucy?"

Lucy: "Well, my brother _____ (go) camping; but I don't like

camping, so I _____ (spend) the weekend at home. I

_____ (go) shopping on Saturday morning and then I

_____ (clean) the house; in the afternoon I

_____ (prepare) a meal, because some friends cf my

parents _____ (visit) us on Saturday evening; they

_____ (stay) overnight and _____ (leave) on

Sunday morning. What _____ you _____ (plan) to do?"

Bob: "Mike and I _____ (go) to an open-air concert on Sunday

afternoon. Two famous pop groups _____ (play) there.

And you _____ (come) with us!"

Lucy: "Why me?"

Bob: "Because it is your birthday on

Sunday, and this is my

birthday present for you."

ICH SPIEL' DA AUCH
AM SONNTAG!

Das Simple Present ist die „Fahrplanzukunft" und steht in Nebensätzen.

Wie im Deutschen verwendest du das **Simple Present:**

▶ um auszudrücken, daß ein **zukünftiges Ereignis bereits festgelegt** ist. Dies gilt besonders bei Fahr- und Zeitplänen, bei Programmen und Veranstaltungen, fast immer in Verbindung mit einer Zeitbestimmung.

> The match **begins** at 4 o'clock.

▶ in Nebensätzen, die durch *when, before, while, as soon as, if* und *until* eingeleitet werden. Im Hauptsatz steht meistens „will".

> I'll do my homework, when I **get** home.

Übungen

▪ Zeitbestimmungen ▪

A Sieh dir die Tafeln an, und bilde Fragen und Antworten dazu. Benutze die folgenden Verben:

leave, start, begin, finish, arrive, open, close, end
Beispiel: When does the plane for Dublin leave?
It leaves at 10.40 and arrives in Dublin at 12.15.

1.

SUMMER TERM
Refresher Course
18th March –
28th July

2.

TRADE FAIR

20th–28th
APRIL

3.

Shop
9 a.m. – 6.30 p.m.

4.

Film
8.15 p.m. – 10.30 p.m.

▪ Bindewörter ▪

Bilde aus zwei Sätzen einen, indem du die Konjunktionen (Binde- **B**
wörter) einsetzt.

1. I'll tell you about my holiday. I'll get back. (when)

When I get back, I'll tell you about my holiday.

2. Anne will go out. She'll have a bath. (before)

_____

3. Mary's husband will be at work. She'll visit friends. (while)

_____

_____

4. I won't start dinner. Peter will arrive. (until)

_____

5. Jack's parents will be happy. He'll pass the exam. (if)

_____

6. Mother won't leave the house. The children will get home. (till)

_____

_____

7. Winter will begin. The birds will fly away. (when)

_____

_____

8. My friend will phone me. She'll arrive in London. (as soon as)

_____

_____

DAS MORGEN GEWINNT KONTUREN
Die Zukunftsformen im Überblick

Du hast nun die fünf verschiedenen Zukunftsformen kennengelernt. Dabei wirst du festgestellt haben, daß es wiederholt mehrere
Möglichkeiten gibt, ein und dasselbe Geschehen darzustellen. Vor
allem die Formen *going to-Future, Future Progressive* und *Present
Progressive* sind in der Verwendung sehr ähnlich und manchmal aus-
tauschbar. Welche Zeitform du wählst, hängt davon ab, wie du das
künftige Geschehen einschätzt (z. B. als Vorhersage, Absicht, festen
Plan).

Die Zukunftsformen auf einen Blick

| will-Future (*I'll leave.*) | Vermutung, Vorhersage (oft mit Signalwörtern) | 1 |
| | spontaner Entschluß, Versprechen | 2 |

| going to-Future (*I'm going to leave.*) | feste Absicht | 3 |
| | kurz bevorstehendes Ereignis (Anzeichen deuten darauf hin) | 4 |

| Future Progressive (*I'll be leaving.*) | Verlauf einer zukünftigen Handlung | 5 |
| | sicher eintretendes Ereignis | 6 |

| Present Progressive (*I'm leaving.*) | fest geplantes Ereignis (oft mit Zeitangabe) | 7 |

| Simple Present (*The train leaves.*) | Programm / Fahrplan | 8 |
| | in Nebensätzen der Zeit und im „if"-Satz (Typ 1) | 9 |

Übungen

■ Blicke in die Zukunft! ■

Gib an, welche Aussagen in den folgenden Sätzen gemacht werden.
Setze die jeweils richtige Zahl (1–9) von der linken Seite in die
blauen Kästchen ein.

A

a. This time next week I'll be lying on the beach.

b. The concert begins at 8 o'clock.

c. The Smiths are having a party next Saturday.

d. You must phone him as soon as you arrive.

e. Look out! The glass is going to fall.

f. There's someone on the phone. Okay, I'll answer it.

g. This summer will be very rainy.

h. Has Tom painted his room yet? No, but he is going to paint it.

i. The plane will be landing in ten minutes.

Landendes
Flugzeug im
Anflug

■ A Trip to New York ■

A   Angela fährt mit ihren Eltern in den Ferien nach New York. Sie erzählt ihrer Freundin Barbara von ihren Reiseplänen.
Setze die Verben in die richtige Zukunftsform. (Es sind zum Teil mehrere Lösungen möglich. Schreibe diese in dein Heft.)

Angela: "I _____ (get) pretty excited about our trip."

Barbara: "I'm sure you are. When _____ you _____ (leave)?"

Angela: "Next Friday. The plane _____ (leave) at 1 p.m. from

Frankfurt and _____ (arrive) at Kennedy Airport at

3 p.m. local time."

Barbara: "Where _____ you _____ (stay)?"

Angela: "We _____ (stay) at a nice hotel near Central Park.

So I _____ (go) for a walk there as soon as we have

checked in, unless I _____ (be) too tired."

Barbara: "What _____ you _____ (do) while you

_____ (be) in N.Y.?"

Angela: "Sightseeing, of course! On Saturday we _____ (walk)

all around Manhattan, because you see most while walking.

We _____ (visit) all the famous buildings as the World

Trade Center, the United Nations Headquarters and, of course,

the Empire State Building. There we _____ (go) to the

top floor – that is the 102nd. Let's hope the weather

_____ (be) clear then, so that we _____ (be

able) to see far into the country. On Saturday we

_____ (take) a boat trip round Manhattan. If we

_____ (have) time we

_____ (go) over to Liberty Island

where the Statue of Liberty

_____ (stand). In the evenings we

_____ (have) dinner in Chinatown

or Greenwich Village. We'd also like to visit a

show on Broadway; but I'm afraid we

_____ (not get) tickets. My parents

_____ (visit) the famous museums, but I don't think I

_____ (go) with them. I suppose I _____

(have) a look round Macy's, the biggest department store in the

world, instead. Maybe I _____ (find) something inter-

esting to buy as a souvenir."

Barbara: "I'm sure you _____ (have) a wonderful holiday."

Angela: "Yes, thanks. I _____ (send) you a postcard from N.Y.

and I _____ (give) you a ring when we

_____ (get) back to tell you

about my adventures."

■ Die passende Zukunftsform ■

B Setze in den folgenden Sätzen die Verben in eine passende Zukunftsform. (Es sind manchmal mehrere Lösungen möglich.)

1. I'm sure you *will help* (help) me with this exercise.

2. I _____ (swim) all day tomorrow.

3. Mary _____ (come) back next Sunday.

4. If the police _____ (catch) the thief

   they _____ arrest him.

5. Anne _____ (read) a lot in her holidays.

6. The Town Council _____ (build) a new school here.

7. I hope it _____ (not be) too difficult to find a job.

8. Tom and Susan _____ (get married) next week.

9. Perhaps he _____ (arrive) in time for lunch.

10. Look at the clouds. It _____ (rain).

11. Jenny and I _____ (go) to the cinema at 7.30 p.m.

12. Bye-bye, I _____ (see) you. Wait a minute,

    I _____ (see) you to the door.

13. The sightseeing tour _____

    (start) at 3 o'clock.

Test

Übersetze die folgenden Sätze:

1. Gehst du heute abend zu Susan's Party?

Do you go in the evening ?

2

2. Wenn du meinen Brief bekommst, bin ich schon in Amerika.

_____

_____ .

2

3. Der Himmel ist schwarz. Es gibt gleich ein Gewitter.

_____ .

2

4. Wer, glaubst du, gewinnt das Spiel?

_____ ?

2

5. Wirst du das alles essen?

_____ ?

2

6. Hältst du bitte meine Pakete, während ich den Schirm öffne?

_____

_____ ?

2

7. Sie sind bis Mittwoch nicht zurück. – Ich sage es ihm.

_____ .

2

8. Kann ich dich morgen nachmittag anrufen?

Nein, dann arbeite ich im Garten.

_____

_____ .

2

Bei weniger als 10 Punkten solltest du die Kapitel zum Thema „Future" von Seite 88 an noch einmal durcharbeiten.

16 Summe

EINLAUF IN DIE ZIELGERADE
Abschlußtests

1 Du hast jetzt die Anwendung aller Zeiten kennengelernt und kannst dein Wissen in diesen Abschlußtests noch einmal überprüfen.

Wähle die richtige Zeit aus, und kreuze an.

1. He _____ football when he fell down.

   a. was playing   b. played   c. has played

2. I _____ of you while you are taking your test.

   a. am thinking   b. think   c. will be thinking

3. The woman was so hungry because she _____ for six days.

   a. didn't eat   b. hadn't eaten   c. hasn't eaten

4. If the weather is fine _____ to the seaside.

   a. we go   b. we'll go   c. we went

5. When _____ you in London?

   a. did   b. have … been   c. were

6. He _____ to hospital yesterday.

   a. went   b. has gone   c. was

7. I _____ tennis next Saturday.

   a. am going to play   b. played   c. play

8. Listen, the band _____ a march now.

   a. plays   b. is playing   c. has played

9. Don't touch anything until the police _____

   a. arrive   b. will arrive   c. arrived

10. I _____ her father since 1980.

    a. am knowing   b. have been knowing   c. have known

11. Where _____ born?

    a. are you   b. have you been   c. were you

12. They sold the house though they _____ in it for 20 years.

    a. have lived   b. had lived   c. lived

13. Please ring me before you _____ the house.

    a. are leaving   b. leave   c. will leave

14. It _____ when we left the house.

    a. has rained   b. rained   c. was raining

15. I _____ at 8 o'clock this morning.

    a. am woken up   b. had woken up   c. woke up

16. Which is the fastest car you _____?

    a. ever drive   b. ever drove   c. have ever driven

17. There is much to do. Don't worry, I _____

    a. will help you   b. help you   c. will you help

18. _____ classical music?

    a. Does Peter like   b. Is Peter liking   c. Likes Peter

19. Six weeks after Tom _____ manager his firm collapsed.

    a. was becoming   b. had become   c. became

20. The police arrested the man who _____ into a shop.

    a. broke   b. had broken   c. has broken

21. The film _____ at 7.30.

    a. is beginning   b. is going to begin   c. begins

2 Jetzt wird es etwas schwieriger. Bilde Sätze oder Fragen. Benutze dabei die richtige Verbform.

1. eat / fish and chips / ever / you?

   _____?

2. Grandpa / in his armchair / sleep / always / TV / he / watch / when.

   _____.

3. find / the doctor / the driver / injured / be / who / seriously / an hour ago.

   _____.

4. which / English grammar / to be easy / at first / seem / more difficult / later on / be.

   _____.

5. spend / in Spain / your / you / last holidays?

   _____?

6. work / in the garden / our neighbour / look.

   _____.

7. tell / nobody / before tomorrow / us / the truth.

   _____.

8. not know / Betty / last English lesson / Scotland / anything / about / in the.

   _____.

9. lie / in Spain / tomorrow / I / this time / on the beach.

   _____.

10. famous / suddenly / after / for several years / be ignored / the author / by the public / he / become.

    _____.

11. one / last Sunday / burst / of my tyres / I / sharp bend / as / round / drive.

_____ .

12. have / more / accident / you / slowly / we / drive / an / if / not.

_____ .

13. Harold / King of England / his / be crowned / authority / in January

1066 / be questioned / when.

_____ .

14. wake up / Sam / usually / in the morning / at 7?

_____ ?

15. take / just a minute / to the post office / I / rain / letter / again /

because / later / it.

_____ .

DANKE, DANKE!
GENUG DER EHRE!

Schreibe die richtigen Verbformen in dein Heft, und erfinde das Ende der Geschichte selbst.

James: Oh hello, Mr Stanley and Miss Sandra. … you … (have) a good trip?
Sandra: Fine, thank you, James. I see the house … (be painted). … you … (hear) anything about our friend Professor Maddock?

James: Professor Maddock? I … (not hear) of him since he … (leave) three weeks ago. He … (tell) me something about a rocket and a flight to the Moon.
Bob Stanley: A flight to the Moon? Crazy. We'll phone him, if we … (know) where he is at the moment. Look, there … (be) a telegram.

OVERSEAS TELEGRAM
am in Cairo – stop – come soon –
need your help – stop – address:
Hilton Palace – stop – Cairo – stop –
Maddock

Four hours later

Sandra: Maddock … (be) in Egypt? What's the crazy fellow doing there? Shall we go?
Bob Stanley: Of course! James, … (take) our suitcases back and … (call) a taxi. We … (leave) now.

Bob Stanley: … (be) there a message for Bob Stanley?
Lady: Yes, sir, here you are.

Bob Stanley: I wonder if Maddock … (be) here to meet us. I … (not see) him anywhere.
Sandra: Perhaps he … (leave) a message at the information desk?

TAKE A TAXI AND COME TO TUTAMALU.
MADDOCK

Sandra: That seems to be very mysterious. Shall we go?
Bob Stanley: Why not? Perhaps he … (need) our help.

Sandra: I ... (watch) that car. It ... (follow) us since we ... (leave) the airport.

Bob Stanley: Don't worry. Look, they ... (turn) to the left.

Bob Stanley: I think we ... (arrive). But what's that? What a big tower.
Sandra: There's Professor Maddock. He ... (come) out of that building.

Professor Maddock: Hello, Miss Sandra and Bob Stanley. I ... (be) really happy to see you here.
Sandra: Professor, what's going on here? Why ... you ... (send) us this puzzling telegram?
Professor Maddock: Just a minute. Follow me to the tower and you ... (see).

Bob Stanley: But what the hell are we to do on the Moon? Please tell us.

Professor Maddock: Every year we … (send) a satellite to the Moon. The same this year. But we … (not hear) from it for three months. It … (be) the most expensive and most important satellite we … (ever build). Now it is lost. It … (land) on the side of the Moon invisible from the Earth, and so it's our task to get into this rocket, to land on the Moon and to find the satellite.

Bob Stanley: What on earth is that?

Professor Maddock: This … (be) a nuclear-powered rocket which is going to take you and me to the Moon.

Sandra: Ha, ha, ha, the Moon. That's a pretty joke. As easy as a pie. I … (not laugh) so much for years.

Professor Maddock: But that's no joke. In half an hour we … (start). Now put on these space suits and let's get in.

Sandra: But why us, Professor?

Professor Maddock: This mission … (be) top secret. And you are my best friends.

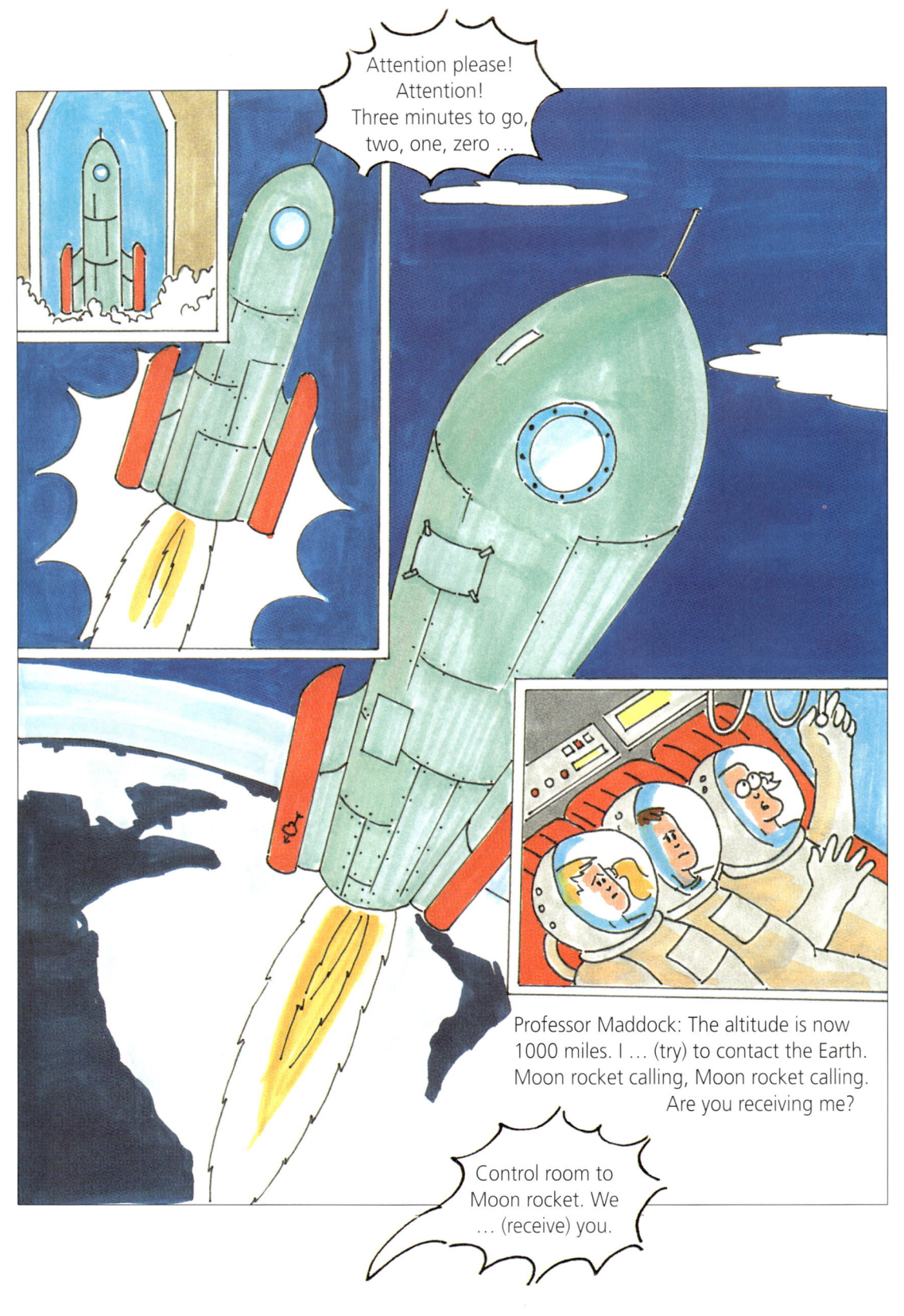

Twenty hours later

Sandra: I … (never see) such a fantastic view.
Professor Maddock: Put on your safety belts.
We … (land) in a few minutes.

Bob Stanley: I … (not see) any signpost. Which direction should we take to find the satellite? Professor Maddock: Ha, ha, ha, a signpost on the Moon. We … (go) straight on to that crater.

to be continued

DIE ZEITEN IM ÜBERBLICK

Simple Form

	Simple Present	Simple Past	Present Perfect Simple
I	work	worked	have worked
you	work	worked	have worked
he/she/it	work**s**	worked	**has** worked
we	work	worked	have worked
you	work	worked	have worked
they	work	worked	have worked

Progressive Form

	Present Progressive	Past Progressive	Present Perfect Progressive
I	am working	was working	have been working
you	are working	were working	have been working
he/she/it	is working	was working	has been working
we	are working	were working	have been working
you	are working	were working	have been working
they	are working	were working	have been working

Simple Form

		Past Perfect	will-Future	going to-Future
I		had worked	will work	am going to work
you		had worked	will work	are going to work
he/she/it		had worked	will work	is going to work
we		had worked	will work	are going to work
you		had worked	will work	are going to work
they		had worked	will work	are going to work

Progressive Form

	Future Progressive
I	will be working
you	will be working
he/she/it	will be working
we	will be working
you	will be working
they	will be working

DIE UNREGELMÄSSIGEN VERBEN

Infinitiv	Simple Past (2. Form)	Past Participle (3. Form)	
be	was / were	been	*sein*
beat	beat	beaten	*schlagen*
become	became	become	*werden*
begin	began	begun	*beginnen*
bite	bit	bitten	*beißen*
break	broke	broken	*brechen*
bring	brought	brought	*bringen*
build	built	built	*bauen*
burn	burnt, burned	burnt, burned	*brennen*
buy	bought	bought	*kaufen*
catch	caught	caught	*fangen*
come	came	come	*kommen*
cost	cost	cost	*kosten*
cut	cut	cut	*schneiden*
do	did	done	*tun*
draw	drew	drawn	*zeichnen*
dream	dreamt, dreamed	dreamt, dreamed	*träumen*
drink	drank	drunk	*trinken*
drive	drove	driven	*fahren*
eat	ate	eaten	*essen*
fall	fell	fallen	*fallen*
feed	fed	fed	*füttern*
fight	fought	fought	*kämpfen*
find	found	found	*finden*
fly	flew	flown	*fliegen*
forget	forgot	forgotten	*vergessen*
freeze	froze	frozen	*frieren*
get	got	got	*bekommen*
give	gave	given	*geben*
go	went	gone	*gehen*
grow	grew	grown	*wachsen*
have	had	had	*haben*
hear	heard	heard	*hören*
hide	hid	hidden	*verstecken*
hold	held	held	*halten*
hurt	hurt	hurt	*verletzen*
keep	kept	kept	*behalten*
know	knew	known	*wissen*
lay	laid	laid	*legen*
lead	led	led	*führen*
leave	left	left	*verlassen*
lend	lent	lent	*leihen*
let	let	let	*zulassen*

Infinitiv	Simple Past (2. Form)	Past Participle (3. Form)	
lie	lay	lain	*liegen*
lose	lost	lost	*verlieren*
make	made	made	*machen*
mean	meant	meant	*bedeuten*
meet	met	met	*treffen*
pay	paid	paid	*bezahlen*
put	put	put	*stellen*
read	read	read	*lesen*
ride	rode	ridden	*reiten*
ring	rang	rung	*klingeln*
run	ran	run	*laufen*
say	said	said	*sagen*
see	saw	seen	*sehen*
sell	sold	sold	*verkaufen*
send	sent	sent	*schicken*
set	set	set	*setzen*
shake	shook	shaken	*schütteln*
shine	shone	shone	*scheinen*
shoot	shot	shot	*schießen*
show	showed	shown	*zeigen*
shut	shut	shut	*schließen*
sing	sang	sung	*singen*
sink	sank	sunk	*sinken*
sit	sat	sat	*sitzen*
sleep	slept	slept	*schlafen*
speak	spoke	spoken	*sprechen*
spend	spent	spent	*verbringen*
spread	spread	spread	*ausbreiten*
stand	stood	stood	*stehen*
steal	stole	stolen	*stehlen*
strike	struck	struck	*schlagen*
swim	swam	swum	*schwimmen*
take	took	taken	*nehmen*
teach	taught	taught	*lehren*
tear	tore	torn	*zerreißen*
tell	told	told	*erzählen*
think	thought	thought	*denken / meinen*
throw	threw	thrown	*werfen*
wake up	woke up	woken up	*aufwachen*
wear	wore	worn	*tragen*
win	won	won	*gewinnen*
write	wrote	written	*schreiben*

LÖSUNGEN

....

Das Simple Present

Seite 11
ÜBUNG: goes / do / eats / get up / try / teaches / reads / play.

Seite 13
ÜBUNG ZUR FRAGEBILDUNG: When does Tom go to school? / Who is the trainer of my football team? / Where does Sandra come from? / Do Paul and Peter often win bicycle races? / Who saves 5 DM every week? / How much does he save? / What do I buy? / Where do I buy a new game for my Game Boy? / When must Christina do her homework? / What must Christina do? / Who washes the car every Saturday? / Does Richard live in a beautiful house? / How old is Tanya?

ÜBUNG ZUR VERNEINUNG: No, my father doesn't work in an office. / No, I'm ... years old. / No, the Queen doesn't live in Australia. / No, Sandra's mother doesn't buy a new car every year. / No, I don't like English very much. / No, I can't go to school in my summer holidays.

Seite 14
MISTER Z: tries / teach / like / write / have / think / November / plays.

EIN INTERVIEW: What's your job, Mr Brown? / Ich arbeite als Lehrer in York. / What do you teach? / Ich unterrichte Englisch und Geschichte. / Do the teachers and pupils have lunch at school? / Oh ja, Lehrer und Schüler essen zu Mittag in der Schule, aber ich nicht. / What do you do in your free time (spare time)? / Ich lese gern Bücher. / Does your wife work, too? / Nein, meine Frau arbeitet nicht. / How do you like Germany? / Mir gefällt Deutschland sehr gut.

Seite 16
DER FRAGEBOGEN: Do you like school? / Do you clean your bike every Saturday? / Do you like this book? / Do you read comics? / Have you got a computer? / Do you have a favourite game? / Do you help at home? / Do you go to school by bus? / Does your mother help you with your homework? / Do you wake up late on Saturdays?

Seite 17
DIE BILDERGESCHICHTE: Peter gets up at 7. Mother makes the breakfast. Peter goes to school by bike. In the afternoon he plays with his friends. In the evening he watches TV. He goes to bed at 9.

EIN BRIEF: So könnte dein Brief aussehen:
Dear Sandra,
My name is Tim Taylor. I live in Düsseldorf. I want to tell you what I usually do.
I always get up at 7 o'clock in the morning. My mother wakes me up. Then I have a shower at 7.15. During this time mother always prepares the breakfast. I usually have breakfast at 7.30. At 7.45 I have to go to school by bus. School always finishes at 13.00. When I come home I usually have lunch. After lunch I must do my homework. My mother always helps me with my homework. Love, ...

Seite 19
TEST: No, the word Jeans doesn't come from French, it comes from English. / No, the word Café doesn't come from Italian, it comes from French. / Does the word Computer come from Spanish? / No, the words Souvenir and Saison don't come from Swedish, they come from French. / Yes, the word Foul comes from Eng-

124

lish. / Does the word Paella come from French? It comes from Spanish. / No, the words Theater and Chemie don't come from Irish, they come from Greek.

Das Present Progressive

Seite 21
ÜBUNG: The mouse is reading. / The mouse is singing. / The mouse is playing. / The mouse is sleeping.

Seite 23
ÜBUNG ZUR FRAGEBILDUNG: Tim, what are you doing? I'm playing in the garden. / Peter, what are you doing? I'm watching TV. / Grandpa, what are you doing? I'm reading a book.

ÜBUNG ZUR VERNEINUNG: 1. I'm not playing with my Game Boy at the moment. / 2. We're not playing football now. / 3. Mother isn't cooking lunch today. / 4. Father and Tom aren't washing the car. / 5. Look, Peter isn't doing his homework. / 6. My parents aren't watching TV at the moment. / 7. The cat isn't eating a mouse. / 8. I'm not cleaning my bike. / 9. The girls aren't singing a song. / 10. Sandra isn't drinking a glass of milk.

Seite 24
DIE BUCHSTABENSUCHE: referring / winning / sitting / stirring / forgetting / putting / running / shutting / cancelling / cutting / getting / travelling.

DIE VERBMASCHINE: 2. they are (they're) swimming / 3. you're buying / 4. we're taking / 5. she's learning / 6. you're teaching / 7. they're looking / 8. he's crying / 9. she's lying / 10. it's coming / 11. we're enjoying / 12. he's hurrying.

Seite 25
EINE LANGWEILIGE HAUSAUFGABE? Who hears a noise? / What does Peter suddenly hear? / Where does he see his mother? / Who is carrying big shopping bags? / What is she carrying? / Is she coming from the shopping centre? / What is Peter doing? / What is Peter taking? / Where is he carrying the shopping bags? / When is David watching TV? / What is David doing an hour later? / Who is still doing his homework? / What is Peter still doing?

Seite 26
FRAGEN ÜBER FRAGEN: 2. Are you helping your mother in the kitchen? / 3. Where are you going just now? / 4. What is Peter doing? / 5. Are you dancing with Paul this evening? / 6. What is the cat doing? / 7. Is Tom playing football with his friends? / 8. Why are the children not playing outside?

BILDERGESCHICHTEN: 2. No, the girl isn't playing ball. She is lying in the sun. / 3. No, they aren't lying in the sun. They are swimming in the sea. / 4. Yes, the man is drinking a glass of beer. / 5. Yes, one of the girls is wearing jeans. / 6. No, the girls aren't carrying shopping bags. They are carrying school bags. / 7. No, the girls aren't at home. They are standing in front of the school. / 8. Yes, one of the girls is laughing.

Seite 27
WINNETOU UND OLD SHATTERHAND: Peter is visiting his friend Tom. "Hi, Tom, what are you doing just now?"
"I'm reading an exciting book by Karl May," Tom answers. "Tell me about the book," Peter says. "I'm on page 250 at the moment. Winnetou and Old Shatterhand are riding into the prairie and fighting against Indians."

"That sounds interesting," says Peter. He asks Tom: "Do you want to come with me? I'm going to the library now." "No, I still have 150 pages to read," Tom answers. Therefore Peter goes to the library alone.

DER RICHTIGE EINSATZ: is / are / are / are / is / is / am / are / am / are.

Simple Present und Present Progressive

Seite 30

TOP TEN: 1. b / 2. c oder d / 3. c / 4. a / 5. d / 6. b / 7. b / 8. c oder d / 9. d / 10. b.

Seite 31

EIN PUZZLE: He's taking the book from the shelf right now. / She always listens to the radio after school. / Sally never washes her blouse in the bathroom. / Look, he's washing his car. / They go to church every Saturday. / Wait, Peter is brushing his teeth at the moment. / They are going to school just now. / Father usually goes to work at 8 o'clock. / Paul is overtaking Bill at the moment. / Mother always buys sausages at the butcher's.

Seite 32

FC Liverpool – FC Bayern München:
is / aren't / are standing / shoots / kicks / plays / is playing / sends / loses / is working / is / scores / wins.

Seite 33

TEST: brushes / go / is walking / is cleaning / rains / looks / like / tastes / are arriving / am going / doesn't do / is sleeping / costs.

Zwischentest I

Seite 34

TEST 1: 1. Who **goes** to school ... / 2. Peter **never does** his ... / 3. right / 4. Mrs Belton's house **is** at the end of the street. / 5. right / 6. Tom and Peter **don't go** swimming. / 7. Last year I **was** in America. / 8. It **seems** ... / 9. right / 10. Karl **is not** ...

Seite 35

TEST 2:
Simple Present

	+	–
you	take	don't take
he / she / it	goes	doesn't go
we	catch	don't catch
you	learn	don't learn
they	think	don't think

Present Progressive

you	are painting	are not painting
he / she / it	is crying	is not crying
we	are lying	are not lying
you	are tidying	are not tidying
they	are stopping	are not stopping

Das Simple Past

Seite 37

ÜBUNGEN: got / was / wanted / had / wasn't / had / put / hid / took / counted / came / was not / shouted / answered / threw / was.

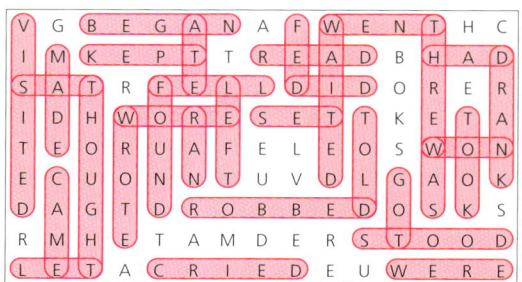

Seite 39

ÜBUNG ZUR RECHTSCHREIBUNG: phoned /
baked / robbed / carried / travelled / cried.

ÜBUNG ZUR FRAGEBILDUNG: When did the
robber arrive? / What did he wear? / What did
he say to the bank clerk? / Who called the
police? / How many people were there in the
bank? / How much did the robber get? / Where
did he go?

Seite 40

ÜBUNG ZUR VERNEINUNG: No, I didn't go
to the cinema last week. / No, I didn't lose my
mother's money. / No, I didn't eat a lot of ice-
cream. / No, I didn't drink five glasses of beer
yesterday. / No, I didn't phone my friend for
one hour.

Seite 41

FEHLENDE VERBEN: 1. played / 2. wrote /
3. catch / 4. got / 5. fight / 6. cleaned / 7. were /
8. did / 9. want.

SOMMERFERIEN: So könnten deine Ge-
schichten aussehen:

1. Our last holiday was wonderful. We had a
lot of sun and fun. We went by car to a nice
camping site. The camping site was at a lake. It
was clean and there was a wood nearby. There
were a lot of other children on the camping
site, too. We played football every day.
I learned to ride and my parents lay on the
beach. We had good food every day.
2. Our last holiday was terrible. It rained all day.
We went by car to a camping site but it was
dirty and noisy. The camping site was far away
from a lake and there were no other children.
We had bad food. When I learned to ride I fell
off the horse and broke my left arm. So I had
to stay in hospital during the last days of the
holiday.

Seite 42

DREI BRIEFE:

1. Aussagesätze

Dear Peter,
Yesterday Sandra phoned me. She wanted to
borrow a book about Robin Hood. She
watched a film about Robin Hood on TV
yesterday and wanted to know more about
him. I thought the book was very interesting
and exciting. Love, …

2. Verneinungen

Dear Sandra,
Yesterday I didn't go to school. I was ill but I
didn't lie in bed. I wanted to read a book but
there wasn't an interesting and exciting one.
My mother and I waited for the doctor. But
Doctor Miller didn't come. Love, …

3. Fragesätze

Dear Petra,
Where did you spend your last summer holidays? Did you go on holiday or did you stay at
home? What did you do the whole day? Did
you read an exciting book? Did it often rain?
Love, …

Seite 43

TEST: 1. Our grandma visited us last week. /
2. She gave me an interesting book about
dinosaurs. / 3. Kate: "Did you go on holiday last
year?" / 4. Pat: "No, we didn't go on holiday." /
5. Kate: "What did you do?" / 6. Pat: "We
often played with the Game Boy when the
weather was bad." / 7. Yesterday evening
Richard went to bed later than his brother. /
8. Last Saturday there was an exciting film
on TV. / 9. In 1990 Germany won the World
Football Championship. / 10. Two hours ago
I did the exercises in this book. They weren't
easy.

Das Past Progressive

Seite 45

WORTFETZEN: 1. When I came home, my parents were reading the newspaper. / 2. While his mother was doing the housework, Peter had to do his homework. / 3. When the postman came, Sandra's dog was barking. / 4. Sam was getting ready for school at eight in the morning when his mother called him. / 5. Tom's father was writing an article for the newspaper all Saturday evening. / 6. Who was driving when the accident happened?

Simple Past und Past Progressive

Seite 47

DIE FOLGEN EINER PARTY: emptied / carried / was doing / cleaned / were hanging up / rang / were getting / heard / thought / were / opened / was laughing / was standing / was getting / came / wanted / was ringing / carried / baked / cleaned / laid / were / was / were looking / was having / was watching / rang / was / told / wanted / started / decided.

Seite 49

TEST: 1. While Guy Fawkes **was** preparing ... / 2. richtig / 3. In 1990 Germany **won** ... / 4. Betty **wanted** to ... / 5. The two men **were drinking** together when they suddenly **started** an argument. / 6. richtig / 7. When the burglar **saw** the police ... / 8. The teacher **knew** his ...

Das Present Perfect Simple

Seite 51

ÜBUNG 1: eat / drink / visit (x) / go / see / drive / cook (x) / carry (x) / write / stop (x) / send / buy.

ÜBUNG 2: 2. has lost / 3. has washed / 4. have lived / 5. has had / 6. has done / 7. has taken off / 8. has cut.

Seite 53

ÜBUNG 1: 1. My father has never been to Australia. / 2. We haven't had dinner yet. / 3. Anne has just read an interesting story. / 4. Have you ever played cricket? / 5. The pupils haven't seen their teacher this morning. / 6. Has Tom cleaned the car yet? / 7. My mother has already made the beds. / 8. The weather has been fine this week.

ÜBUNG 2: Freddy: "No, I haven't tidied my room yet." Mother: "And what about the lunch?" Freddy: "Yes, I have already cooked lunch." Mother: "Have you cleaned the shoes?" Freddy: "No, I haven't done it yet." Mother: "Have you finished your homework?" Freddy: "No, I haven't finished my homework yet." Mother: "And what about the dog?" Freddy: "I have already taken it out."

Seite 54

ÜBUNG: 1. since / 2. for / 3. for / 4. since / 5. since / 6. for / 7. for / 8. since / 9. since / 10. for / 11. for / 12. since.

Seite 55

DEIN TAGEBUCH:

So könnte dein Tagebucheintrag lauten: It has been a busy day. I have already done my homework and I have been shopping in the supermarket. I have also fed my budgie and I have bought stamps at the office; but I haven't cleaned my father's car yet and I haven't tidied my room. I'll have to do that tomorrow because I'm tired now.

STECKVERBINDUNGEN: 2 – c / 3 – e / 4 – a / 5 – d / 6 – f.

Seite 56

EIN RÄTSEL:

1. seen	8. ridden
2. spent	9. rang
3. took	10. win
4. break	11. given
5. eaten	12. lose
6. sang	13. done
7. spoken	14. driven

Seite 57

EINE ANSICHTSKARTE: for / since / for / since / for / for / since / for.

Seite 58

VISITING LONDON: have been / for / since / have you ever been / have you done / I have already visited / I have taken / have you seen / I haven't had / I haven't heard / I have already climbed / I have walked / I have looked / I have already listened / I have never heard / have you ever travelled / I have also been / have you ever met / we have often seen.

Seite 60

EIN ZEITUNGSARTIKEL: has just happened / have already been / have written / have asked / haven't answered / have done / has come.

Seite 61

TEST: 1. My brother has just left the house. / 2. Have you phoned Anne yet? / 3. How long have you known your friend? I have known him since kindergarten. / 4. Tom has not been to a rock concert yet. / 5. We have had our car for five years now. / 6. Mr Miller has already written six letters. / 7. My grandfather has never

travelled to England. / 8. The weather has been fine all week. / 9. Why is your father so tired? He has worked all day. / 10. You have just done the test. Now you can play.

Das Present Perfect Progressive

Seite 63

ÜBUNG: Sue has been listening to music for two hours. / Philip has been reading comics for 15 minutes. / Peter has been swimming since 11.40. / Mike has been eating for 35 minutes. / Jenny has been writing a letter since 12.30. / Billy and Linda have been cleaning the window for 20 minutes.

Present Perfect Simple und Progressive

Seite 65

RICHTIG UND FALSCH: 1. has found / 2. has been working / 3. have broken / 4. have you had / 5. have visited / 6. have been travelling / 7. has cut / 8. have you heard / 9. has she spent / 10. have you been reading / 11. has been playing / has never won / 12. has given up.

Seite 66

INTERVIEW MIT EINEM POPSTAR: have been working / have already produced / have won / have been writing / have been drinking / have smoked / haven't seen / have been living / have just come / have travelled / have been enjoying / have been waiting.

Seite 67

TEST: 1. My brother has been studying languages at the university for two years. / 2. My mother has been cleaning the windows since 10 o'clock. / 3. The tennis star has been playing tennis since he was ten. He has already won Wimbledon four times. / 4. How long have your parents been married? / 5. Billy has been working in London for six years, but he has already changed his job three times. / 6. Why are your hands so dirty? I have just been repairing my car. / 7. It has been snowing for days and it has already snowed 50 cm. / 8. My friend has been looking for his book since 5 o'clock but he hasn't found it yet.

Past Tense und Present Perfect

Seite 69

DER „LÜCKENFÜLLER"-TEST: 1. has been playing / 2. wrote / 3. have you ever broken / 4. has Anne been watching / 5. did Columbus discover / 6. bought / 7. have you seen / 8. has never been / 9. have you had / 10. had.

Seite 70

PAST TENSE ODER PRESENT PERFECT? has just celebrated / was / was / moved / has been living / was working / met / married / died / has never married / had / hasn't been / has never smoked / has been riding / was / has read / hasn't missed / has had.

Seite 71

TEST: 1. When did the train arrive? It has just arrived. / 2. Have you ever been to Italy? Yes, we spent our last holidays there. / 3. My cousin moved to Australia a year ago and he hasn't seen a kangaroo yet. / 4. Were you watching TV when I phoned you yesterday? / 5. Has the postman been here yet? Yes, he was here five minutes ago. / 6. Lizzy has been in hospital for five days now. She broke her leg last week. / 7. When did you last meet Alex? I haven't seen him for a week. / 8. Two months ago my father bought a car and has already driven 2000 km. / 9. Yesterday evening there was a thunderstorm and it has been raining ever since. / 10. Have you done your homework yet? Yes, I did it an hour ago.

Zwischentest II

Seite 72

TEST 1: 1. am thinking / do you think / 2. do you hear / is coming / 3. have / 4. is waiting / 5. does / 6. is raining / don't have (haven't got).

Seite 73

TEST 2: 1. was hunting / hit / 2. woke up / were reading / 3. washed / painted / cut / bought / 4. seemed / had / 5. discovered / were / 6. rang / was watching TV / 7. was / were fighting / 8. was reading / came in.

Seite 74

TEST 3: 1. had / has been shining / 2. haven't seen / told / 3. Have you seen / haven't / 4. have you had / 5. visited / 6. Have you heard / 7. was elected / 8. has stolen.

Seite 75

TEST 4: have you been doing / moved / haven't finished / was painting / came in / told / had to / has been raining / haven't been able to / was sleeping / was / woke up / wasn't able to / was.

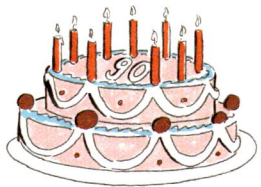

Das Past Perfect

Seite 77

EIN TAG MIT DEN MILLERS: After Mrs Miller had done the dishes, she went shopping. / After Mr Miller had repaired his bike, he went by bike to town. / After Mrs Miller had taken a photo, she went in. / After Mr and Mrs Miller had played cards, they watched TV. / After Mr Miller had gone to bed, he dreamt about his beautiful wife.

Seite 79

PARIS: 2. After they had taken a taxi to their hotel, they enjoyed the view from the Eiffel Tower. / 3. After they had enjoyed the view from the Eiffel Tower, they made a sightseeing tour to Versailles. / 4. After they had made a sightseeing tour to Versailles, they went on a boat trip on the Seine. / 5. After they had gone on a boat trip on the Seine, they visited the Louvre. / 6. After they had visited the Louvre, they took pictures of Paris. / 7. After they had taken pictures of Paris, they returned to their hotel.

Seite 80

DIE QUAL DER WAHL: 1. came out / had expected / 2. stayed / arrived / 3. found / had lost / 4. was / had not expected / 5. didn't understand / had got / 6. hadn't locked / left / 7. seemed / had been shown / 8. had returned / washed / 9. did … break out?

Seite 81

EIN RÄTSEL: 1. had **b**ought / 2. had spr**e**ad / 3. had expl**a**ined / 4. had b**u**rnt / 5. had bi**t**ten / 6. had r**i**dden / 7. had **f**ought / 8. had s**u**nk / 9. had **l**ost.
Lösungswort: beautiful

Seite 82

EIN FEHLERTEXT: 1. Yesterday when Mr Smith arrived home, his wife had already done the shopping. / 2. The door bell rang while Mr Miller was having a shower. / 3. When Bob came to the bus stop, the bus had already left. / 4. richtig / 5. After Tom had arrived home, he watched TV. / 6. I looked at our house which we had sold ten years earlier.

Seite 83

TEST:

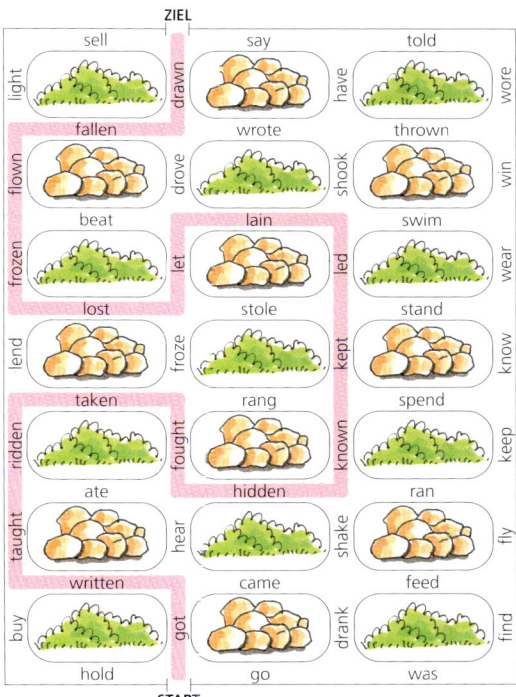

Seite 84
PAST TENSE, PRESENT PERFECT ODER PAST PERFECT? 1. met / was dancing / 2. has not shone / 3. started / had fastened / 4. has been sleeping / 5. have you already been waiting / 6. had died / became / 7. became / had been executed / 8. have you already seen / 9. were / decided.

Seite 85
BESUCH VOM MARS: was / were sitting / were waiting / were looking forward to / didn't start / heard / were beginning / broke / has just noticed / has landed / have already been killed / have come / was continued / ordered / was told / thought / had come true / were running / were crying / were shouting / were searching / had been / became / hasn't been forgotten.

Seite 86
FINDE DEN TÄTER! were standing / had called / arrived / wanted / entered / saw / were sitting / talking / said / has happened / came / started / saw / thought / hadn't locked / left / went / saw / had called / waited / have been stolen / were invited / hadn't said / asked / told / replied / were / danced / was talking / came / had entered / saw / phoned / did you wear / were / had / stole.

Der Täter ist natürlich Peter Higgins. Er trägt als einziger Turnschuhe und hat die Party verlassen, um den Schmuck und die Juwelen zu stehlen. Als er nach dem Diebstahl auf die Party zurückging, vergaß er, die Schuhe zu wechseln.

Seite 89
ÜBUNG: 2. you won't lose / 3. you won't get / 4. you'll be / 5. you'll meet / 6. your team will win / 7. it won't rain.

Seite 90
SCHEINBARE PAARE: 1 – b / 2 – a / 3 – b / 4 – a / 5 – b / 6 – b / 7 – a / 8 – b.
BLICK IN DIE ZUKUNFT: 1. will, will, won't, will / 2. Will people work harder? / won't, will, won't, will / 3. Will people have more free time? / will, will, will, won't, will / 4. Will people be happier? / will, will, will, won't, will, won't.

Seite 93
ÜBUNG: 1. Frank is going to play football. / 2. Lucy is going to read. / 3. Peggy and Jenny are going camping. / 4. Susan is going to ride a horse.

Seite 94
„WILL" ODER „GOING TO"? 1. I'm going to / 2. I'll do / 3. won't be / 4. he isn't going to / 5. will … say / 6. I'll have / 7. Tom will get / 8. it'll break / 9. he is going to / 10. I'll cut / 11. will / 12. are you going to buy / will you buy.

Seite 95
ZUKUNFTSPLÄNE: I'm going to become / I'll go / is going to study / I'm going to work / I'll have to work / I'll learn / are going to start / we'll open / will lend / I'm going to marry / is going to become / will probably work / I'll see.

Das Future Progressive

Seite 97
ÜBUNG: 2. Between 10.30 a.m. – 11.30 a.m. he'll be visiting / 3. At 1 p.m. he'll be having lunch / 4. From 2 p.m. – 4 p.m. he'll be discussing / 5. At 5 p.m. he'll be having / 6. At 8.30 p.m. he'll be leaving.

Präsensformen mit zukünftiger Bedeutung

Seite 98
SATZBAU: 2. My sister is getting married in August. / 3. Is your brother going to Paris tomorrow? / 4. Henry is playing tennis with Anne this afternoon. / 5. He's leaving for Hamburg next week. / 6. We are not watching TV tonight. / 7. My uncle is coming to see us next Friday. / 8. You are not going on holiday this summer. / 9. We are doing our English homework in an hour's time.

Seite 99
WOCHENENDPLÄNE: are you doing / is going / I'm spending / I'm going / I'm cleaning / I'm preparing / are visiting / are staying / are leaving / are you planning / are going / are playing / are coming.

Seite 100
ZEITBESTIMMUNGEN: 1. When does the summer term start (begin)? It starts (begins) on 18th March and ends (finishes) on 28th July. / 2. When does the trade fair begin (start)? It begins (starts) on 20th April and finishes (ends) on 28th April. / 3. When does the shop open? It opens at 9 a.m. and closes at 6.30 p.m. / 4. When does the film begin (start)? It begins (starts) at 8.15 p.m. and ends (finishes) at 10.30 p.m.

Seite 101
BINDEWÖRTER: 2. Anne will have a bath before she goes out. / 3. Mary will visit friends while her husband is at work. / 4. I won't start dinner until Peter arrives. / 5. Jack's parents will be happy if he passes the exam. / 6. Mother won't leave the house till the children get home. / 7. When winter begins the birds will fly away. / 8. My friend will phone me as soon as she arrives in London.

Die Zukunftsformen im Überblick

Seite 103
BLICKE IN DIE ZUKUNFT! a – 5 / b – 8 / c – 7 / d – 9 / e – 4 / f – 2 / g – 1 / h – 3 / i – 6.

Seite 104
A TRIP TO NEW YORK: **A.:** I'm getting / **B.:** are you leaving – are you going to leave – will you be leaving / **A.:** leaves / arrives / **B.:** are you staying – are you going to – will you stay / **A.:** will be staying – will stay / I'll go / I am / **B.:** are you going to do – will you be doing / you are / **A.:** we are going to / are going to visit – are visiting / are going / will be / will be able / we are taking – going to take / have / we'll go / stands / will be having – will have – are going to have / we won't get / are going to visit / I will go / I'll have / I'll find / **B.:** you'll have / **A.:** I'll send / I'll give / get.

Seite 106
DIE PASSENDE ZUKUNFTSFORM: 2. will be swimming / 3. is coming / 4. catch / will / 5. is going to / 6. is going to – will build – will be building / 7. won't / 8. are getting – are going to get / 9. will / 10. is going to / 11. are going / 12. will be seeing / I'll see / 13. starts.

Seite 107

TEST: 1. Are you going to Susan's party tonight?/2. When you get my letter I'll already be in America./3. The sky is black. There is going to be a thunderstorm./4. Who do you think will win the match?/5. Are you going to eat that all?/6. Will you hold my parcels, please, while I open the umbrella?/7. They won't be back until Wednesday. – I'll tell him./8. Can I call you tomorrow afternoon? No, I will be working in the garden then.

Abschlußtests

Seite 108

TEST 1: 1a/2c/3b/4b/5c/6a/7a/8b/9a/10c/11c/12b/13b/14c/15c/16c/17a/18a/19b/20b/21c.

Seite 110

TEST 2: 1. Have you ever eaten fish and chips?/2. Grandpa always sleeps in his armchair when he watches TV./3. The doctor found the driver who had been seriously injured an hour ago./4. English grammar, which seems to be easy at first, will be more difficult later on./5. Did you spend your last holidays in Spain?/6. Look, our neighbour is working in the garden./7. Nobody will tell us the truth before tomorrow./8. Betty didn't know anything about Scotland in the last English lesson./9. This time tomorrow I will be lying on the beach in Spain./10. The author suddenly became famous after he had been ignored by the public for several years./11. As I was driving round a sharp bend last Sunday one of my tyres burst./12. If you don't drive more slowly we'll have an accident./13. When Harold was crowned King of England in January 1066 his authority was questioned./14. Does Sam usually wake up at 7 in the morning?/15. Just

a minute! Because it is raining again I'll take the letter to the post office later.

Seite 112

FLIGHT TO THE MOON:

Bild 2: did you have/has been painted/have you heard.
Bild 3: haven't heard/left/told/know/is.

Seite 114

Bild 5: is/take/call/are leaving.
Bild 7: is/don't see/has left.
Bild 8: is.
Bild 10: needs.

Seite 116

Bild 11: am watching/has been following/left.
Bild 12: are turning.
Bild 14: have arrived/is coming.
Bild 15: am/did you send/will see.
Bild 16: is/haven't laughed/are starting.
Bild 17: send/haven't heard/was/have ever built/landed.
Bild 18: is.

Seite 118

Bild 22: will try/are receiving.
Bild 23: have never seen/will be landing.
Bild 25: don't see/will go.

BYE-BYE! BIS ZUM NÄCHSTEN MAL!

In der Reihe FALKEN Schülerhilfe sind zahlreiche Titel erschienen.
Bitte fragen Sie in Ihrer Buchhandlung.

ISBN 3 8068 1574 7

Umschlaggestaltung: Peter Udo Pinzer
Gestaltung: Horst Bachmann
Redaktion: Dr. Werner Brand
Herstellung: Harald Kraft
Titelgrafiken: Jovica Savin, Frankfurt am Main
Fotos: adidas, Herzogenaurach: 32/33; **Bongarts**, Hamburg: 32 (Beate Müller), 43, 49; **dpa**, Frankfurt
am Main: 5 M.l., 14 (Gutberlet), 15 o. (Camera Press), 15 u. (Scholz); **G. Kelbert**, Idstein: 48, 82, 86;
Lufthansa-Bildarchiv, Frankfurt am Main: 5 u.r., 97; **Ulrich Niehoff**, Bienenbüttel: 6, 25, 47 u., 66;
Silvestris Fotoservice, Kastl/Obb.: 56, 57, 60; 4 o., 58 o.l. (Beck); 58 M.r., u.l. (Robert Harding); 59,
108 (Ladislav Janicek); 103 (Kuchelbauer Josef); 79, 105 (The Telegraph Colour Library); 104/105
(Maximilian Weinzierl); **FALKEN Archiv:** 47 o., 91; Danilo Lex: 89 o.r., M.u.l.; Nadolny: 89 o.l., M.r.;
Pinzer: 42, 95; Rodenstock/Pinzer: 69 u.; Pool Ges./Hogen u. Zöltsch: 89 u.r.; Röltsch: 89 M.o.l., u.l.;
TLC: 29; M. Zorn: 27
Zeichnungen: Jovica Savin, Frankfurt am Main; außer: **Anke Lintz**, Ingelheim am Rhein: 53;
Daniela Schneider, Frankfurt am Main: 18 o.; **Atelier Schneider & Hinz**, Hannover: 69 o.

Die Ratschläge in diesem Buch sind von den Autoren und vom Verlag sorgfältig erwogen und geprüft,
dennoch kann eine Garantie nicht übernommen werden. Eine Haftung der Autoren bzw. des Verlags und
seiner Beauftragten für Personen-, Sach- und Vermögensschäden ist ausgeschlossen.

Satz: Raasch & Partner GmbH, Neu-Isenburg
Druck: Ludwig Auer GmbH, Donauwörth

817 2635 4453

Schulsorgen?

Neben dieser Buchreihe bietet die Schülerhilfe, Deutschlands große Nachhilfe-Organisation, einen regelmäßigen Förderunterricht. Dort gibt's qualifizierte Hausaufgaben-Betreuung in kleinen Gruppen und preiswerte Nachhilfe ab der Grundschule. Schülerhilfen finden Sie in vielen deutschen Städten.

Wählen Sie unsere bundeseinheitliche Telefon-Nr. 19 418 montags bis freitags von 15.00 bis 17.30 Uhr.

(Ganztagsauskunft unter 0209/19 418)